A CUP OF CAPPUCCINO
FOR THE ENTREPRENEUR'S SPIRIT™

Love & Thanks
Kayhan

A CUP OF CAPPUCCINO
FOR THE ENTREPRENEUR'S SPIRIT™

find your passion and live the dream™

VOLUME I

ENTREPRENEURS' STORIES TO INSPIRE AND
ENERGIZE YOUR ENTREPRENEURIAL SPIRIT

JERETTA HORN NORD

Copyright © 2009 by Jeretta Horn Nord, Entrepreneur Enterprises LLC

Library of Congress Control Number: 2009904869
ISBN: Hardcover 978-1-4415-3733-1
Softcover 978-1-4415-3732-4

All rights reserved. No part of this book may be reproduced or transmitted in any form or by any means, electronic or mechanical, including photocopying, recording, or by any information storage and retrieval system, without permission in writing from the copyright owner.

This book was printed in the United States of America.

Cover design by Karen Lemley

To order additional copies of this book, contact:
Xlibris Corporation
1-888-795-4274
www.Xlibris.com
Orders@Xlibris.com
57514

CONTENTS

Introduction 11
Acknowledgments 15
Submit Your Story 19

CHAPTER ONE: FINDING YOUR PASSION 21

My Journey from Serial Entrepreneur to Social Entrepreneur
  Peter H. Thomas 23
Entrepreneurship Is a Team Sport *Joe Eastin* 29
From Passion and Persistence to Purpose and Prosperity
  Michael Simmons and Sheena Lindahl 35
Chance: Golf Game and a Tornado *Jeff Smith* 40
Life Strategist *Elizabeth Grace Saunders* 45
The Foot Doctor *Rocky Willingham*
  contributed by *Matt Fodge* 49

CHAPTER TWO: LIVING THE DREAM 53

Alive and Well and Livin' the Dream *Ty England* 55
Staying Power *Kayhan Hellriegel* 61
Living the American Dream *Adel Nasreddine* 67
Catching the Entrepreneurial Spirit: Dreams Do Come True
  Mark A. Stansberry 72
Living with an Entrepreneur *Nancy Stansberry* 75
Ropin' the Dream *Ruth Lance Wester and June Proctor* 78

CHAPTER THREE: FINDING A NICHE 81

The Rugged Entrepreneur *Billy Reedy*
    contributed by Justin Hayward 83
Cleaning Up! *Dominic Coryell*... 86
Building a Big, Miniature Empire *Craig Martyn*......................... 90
H Is for Honesty *Emily Pilloton*
    contributed by Elisabeth Garson 95
A Strong Heart and a "Never Quit" Attitude *Lee Roberts*........ 100
The Accidental Entrepreneur *C. Renzi Stone*......................... 104

CHAPTER FOUR: TAKING ACTION.................................. 107

A True Entrepreneur *Charlie Eitel*.. 109
Dr. K *Donald F. Kuratko* 113
Do What You Want *Jack Allen*... 119
Two Phone Calls That Changed My Life *Rocky Marshall*...... 124
Dot-Com Millionaire by Age Nineteen *Kieran O'Neill*............. 128
Success Comes with Responsibility *Joe Alcorn*
    contributed by Stevan J. Alcorn.. 134

CHAPTER FIVE: NETWORKING AND RELATIONSHIPS ... 139

Entrepreneurship in the Twenty-First Century
    Evelyn Echols.. 141
I Was Born with a Gift *Luann Y. Hughes* 145
My Willful Endeavor *Mark Marney*
    contributed by Karin Kinnerud... 150
Enjoying Life! *Cheryl Schreiner*
    contributed by Adam Williams.. 155
The Hot Mommas® Project—Need I Say More?
    Kathy Korman Frey 159

CHAPTER SIX: IT'S ALL ABOUT THE SERVICE 163

We Did It Our Way *Joseph A. Pascaretta
  and Aaron D. Dowen* 165
A Cut above the Others *Jesse Stewart
  contributed by Jocelyn Markert* 171
A Balanced Life *C. C. Crane
  contributed by Heather Arena* 175
Breaking the Barriers *Marilyn Ihloff
  contributed by Amber Baldwin* 179
Building a Reputation of Excellence *Reuben Trevino
  contributed by Jackie Legg Sartin* 184

CHAPTER SEVEN: OVERCOMING THE UNEXPECTED 187

Entrepreneur4Life *Nate Waters* 189
Happiness *Jennifer Horn Hillburn* 195
Building a Life *Jeff Davis contributed by Sydney Davis* 199
Laid Off—No Longer an Option *Katherine E. Sansone* 202
Cars Are Just a Guy Thing—Not! *David Miller II
  contributed by Christina Ikard* 206

CHAPTER EIGHT: IT'S ALL IN THE FAMILY 213

A Thousand Dollars and a Kitchen Table *Lewis B. Ketchum
  contributed by Callie Ketchum* 215
Family First *JJ Miller contributed by Pernilla Lindberg* 221
Cappuccino with a Heart *Tamara Dujmovic* 225
When the Water Flows, So Does the Cash *James Redding
  contributed by Jamie Thompson* 229
A Global Entrepreneur *Martin Hilti
  contributed by Brian Inman* 233

CHAPTER NINE: KNOWLEDGE THROUGH EXPERIENCE.....237

Things They Never Tell You about Owning Your
    Own Business *Vince Orza*... 239
From No Street to Wall Street *Bob Rader* 243
One Simple Beginning to Three Extraordinary Careers
    Fran Jabara contributed by Mary Marshall...................... 247
Rules for Life as an Entrepreneur *John A. Brock*................. 251
No More Chasing the Carrot *Pete and Kimberly Coppola*..... 255

CHAPTER TEN: PERSEVERANCE IS THE KEY.................. 259

He Had Clients—I Had Credit *Sharla J. Frost*....................... 261
The Head and the Heart of the Entrepreneur
    Scott Klososky.. 265
Living with the Entrepreneurial Bug *William Fikhman* 269
It Happens Because I Say So *Louis Lautman*...................... 276
Keep Swinging—An Entrepreneur's Story of Overcoming
    Adversity and Achieving Small Business Success
    Jay B. Myers.. 280

Key Success Factors... 283

Recommended Books 284

Watch for Volume II of *A Cup Of Cappuccino for the
    Entrepreneur's Spirit* 285

Helping First-Generation Entrepreneurs................................. 286

To all who have found their passion and are living the dream

and to all who aspire to

live the entrepreneurial dream.

INTRODUCTION

Entrepreneurship provides jobs, creates and uses goods and services, and stimulates the economy. The world of entrepreneurship is one of excitement, challenges, and rewards, with three out of four Americans aspiring at some point in their lives to be entrepreneurs. Among this majority, at the age of twelve, I rode my bicycle from house to house selling greeting cards and stationery in the rural community where I was raised. This venture prompted my first bank loan—to pay for the products until I could collect from the buyers upon delivery. I didn't know the word at the time, but this was my first experience as an entrepreneur. While pursuing the degrees required for a career as a professor, I engaged in entrepreneurial ventures in real estate, nutritional supplements, and personalized birthday cards. I also enjoyed a twelve-year venture as owner of a hair-and-nail salon.

Following my service on the faculty and as Associate Dean in the Spears School of Business at Oklahoma State University, I had the opportunity to coordinate an Entrepreneurship Speakers Series course. Each semester, approximately twenty entrepreneurs from a diverse range of businesses spoke to a class of 150 students, sharing their stories and advice. I learned from them and became inspired along with the students.

After attending seminars and conferences, where I had the opportunity to hear more entrepreneurs, I asked myself, *What can I do to give everyone an opportunity to receive the inspiration and education I have received from listening to over one hundred entrepreneurs share their stories?* On a flight from New York, it came to me! I would create a series of books of entrepreneurs' stories that include adversities, challenges, triumphs, and successes. To provide even more value, I would ask the entrepreneurs to include key success factors, their Web sites, and recommended books. That very evening, I began the steps that would lead to publishing success stories from entrepreneurs all over the world.

As an entrepreneur with great passion and a real sense of urgency, I developed a business plan, a feasibility study, and a book proposal. I designed the cover, formed a company (Entrepreneur Enterprises LLC), trademarked the book name and logo, developed guidelines and interview questions, made a list of hundreds of entrepreneurs, and requested their stories. Less than nine months from the conception of this idea, *A Cup of Cappuccino for the Entrepreneur's Spirit* Volume I is released. Volumes II and III, as well as Editions for Women, Internet, Global, Social, Eco, Disabled, Native American, Hispanic, African American, and Australian entrepreneurs are in progress; and with your interest, there will be many more editions.

Fifty-eight amazing entrepreneurs from five countries and eighteen states within the USA are featured in Volume I of *A Cup of Cappuccino for the Entrepreneur's Spirit.* Stories included are from numerous types of entrepreneurs ranging in age from twenty-one to ninety-four, with varying goals and income levels. All stories have the common thread of being presented from the entrepreneur's point of view with passion and enthusiasm. You will learn from reading this book that your thoughts and actions can bring you success. These stories will instill in your mind the importance of passion and perseverance and will help you achieve in a way you never thought possible. You can have whatever you want in life if you (1) know what you want, (2) have the passion to go after it, and (3) apply the lessons you will learn in the following entrepreneurs' stories. My intention in creating *A Cup of Cappuccino for the Entrepreneur's Spirit* is for it to bring inspiration, motivation, and knowledge to entrepreneurs and aspiring entrepreneurs worldwide.

I hope *you* not only enjoy reading these stories but learn from them as well, become inspired, and *find your passion and live the dream.*

ACKNOWLEDGMENTS

With sincere appreciation, I thank every individual who has been a part of my life and who has taught, inspired, and energized me through their wisdom and passion.

I especially acknowledge and extend my gratitude to the following individuals who helped make this book possible:

Entrepreneurs who contributed their stories so that those who are entrepreneurs or aspire to be entrepreneurs can learn from, and be inspired by, the best.

Contributors who found entrepreneurs with stories appropriate for this book. Without your contributions, I may not have known these outstanding entrepreneurs or have had the opportunity to share their stories.

My family, who rocks my world:

My husband, Daryl, and my son, Nicholas, for their love and never-ending support. Thank you!

Molly, who has been supportive throughout the creation of this book and who has been a sweetheart to Nicholas.

My superchildren—Jason and his wife, Jenny; Rebecca and her husband, Jon; and Audrey—for accepting me as part of their family and allowing me to substitute *super* for *step*. And Patrick for making Audrey laugh and for his support.

My dad and his wife, Alene, for being great role models and loving parents. My mother, who went to Heaven in 2000, for being my best friend, a wonderful listener, and my greatest fan ever.

My sister, Jennifer, and her husband, Hi, whose love has meant the world to me over the years. My niece Heather and her husband, David, who are extreme entrepreneurs and truly live the dream. Jack, the youngest entrepreneur of our family, and my nephew Jared, who is loved not only by me but by everyone else.

My brother, Jeff, and his wife, Jada, who are both entrepreneurs and love living the life of entrepreneurs. My niece Chelsey and her husband, Jeremy, who are both brilliant, and my nephew Chase and the one who makes him smile, Elise.

My friends Shelby Clanahan, Susan Zimmerman, Heather Arena, Cindy Thompson, Jan McVicker, and Melinda Johnson, who believe in me and make me laugh. Your support has been invaluable, and I treasure our friendship.

Dr. Glenn Freedman for his insight, wisdom, and invaluable advice.

Matthew Winton for his competent handling of the legal aspects of *A Cup of Cappuccino for the Entrepreneur's Spirit.*

Karen Lemley for her contribution to the book cover design.

Sarah Little and Matt Miller for design and production of promotional materials.

Frances Griffin for copyediting and for her professionalism.

Dean Sara Freedman for her support, encouragement, and enthusiasm.

Dr. Rick Wilson for encouraging me to excel in my own way and for his continued support.

Dr. Michael Morris and Nola Miyasaki for developing a world-class entrepreneurship program at Oklahoma State University, and to all academic entrepreneurs who provide a foundation for tomorrow's entrepreneurs.

Dr. Julie Weathers and Vickie Karns for their interest in and support of *A Cup of Cappuccino for the Entrepreneur's Spirit.*

Lou Kerr for her enthusiasm, support, passion, and inspiration to me and to many others.

Randy and Cindy Thompson for their expertise and advice.

The associates at Xlibris Publishing for transforming Volume I of *A Cup of Cappuccino for the Entrepreneur's Spirit* into a marketable reality.

And finally, to all entrepreneurs who have shared their stories as speakers or in writing, for helping me and others realize each setback brings you one step closer to success, and with passion, perseverance, integrity, and hard work, one can truly live the entrepreneurial dream!

SUBMIT YOUR STORY

A Cup of Cappuccino for the Entrepreneur's Spirit features a series of books of entrepreneurs' true stories written to inspire, energize, and teach the reader. The stories include adversities, challenges, triumphs, and successes experienced by the entrepreneur to help readers discover passion and basic principles they can use to live the entrepreneurial dream.

The series will include Volumes I, II, and III of *A Cup of Cappuccino for the Entrepreneur's Spirit* and editions including a Women Entrepreneurs' Edition, an Internet Entrepreneurs' Edition, a Global Entrepreneurs' Edition, an Ecopreneurs' Edition, a Social Entrepreneurs' Edition, a Disabled Entrepreneurs' Edition, a Native American Entrepreneurs' Edition, a Hispanic Entrepreneurs' Edition, an African American Entrepreneurs' Edition, an Australian Entrepreneurs' Edition, and others.

The format and guidelines for writing a story are located on my Web site at *www.acupofcappuccino.com*. Just click on Submit Story.

After reviewing the guidelines, please submit your story as a Microsoft Word document attached to an e-mail to jeretta@acupofcappuccino.com.

Jeretta Horn Nord, Founder and CEO
Entrepreneur Enterprises LLC
A Cup of Cappuccino for the Entrepreneur's Spirit
601 S. Washington #105
Stillwater, OK 74074
405-747-0320
405-743-4802 (fax)

Enjoy, get inspired, and learn from the best as you read the following stories.

CHAPTER ONE

FINDING YOUR PASSION

> *Don't ask yourself what the world needs; ask yourself what makes you come alive. And then go and do that. Because what the world needs is people who have come alive.*
>
> —*Howard Thurman*

The most beautiful things in the world are not seen nor touched. They are felt with the heart.
—*Helen Keller*

MY JOURNEY FROM SERIAL ENTREPRENEUR TO SOCIAL ENTREPRENEUR

For most of my life, I've been a consummate deal maker and a passionate entrepreneur. I started in business as a mutual fund salesman in my midtwenties, which launched me into a thirty-year sales career in investment and real estate across North America. I've lived through four recessions and seen my net worth in the '80s drop from $150 million to a negative $70 million within a few days, yet I persevered through all the ups and downs. What kept me on track through all of the chaos and successes I experienced in life was my entrepreneurial spirit and a can-do attitude, approaching every challenge with the motto, "It's easy; it's a piece of cake!" However, I owe much of my success to understanding the philosophy of living my life in accordance with my values.

It started in my early thirties when I attended a Young Presidents' Organization university class in Hawaii taught by Red Scott. It was a warm, sunny day and Mr. Scott decided to move the class to the beach. There, he asked us to make a list of our values and a list of our daily activities. He then asked us to align the two lists to see how many of our activities reflected our values. This was a huge wake-up call for me—I had an epiphany! I realized most of what I was doing did not align with my core values. I learned the power of recognizing what is important to me in life and setting priorities in accordance with my values—and I never looked back. I strived to live my life in alignment with my values every single day.

It was also during that time in Hawaii that one of my colleagues pointed out the Century 21 Real Estate franchise opportunity. "Hey, Peter," he said, "you seem to be a franchise kind of guy. Why don't you go and check it out." So I did and ended up buying the rights to Century 21 Real Estate in Canada for $100,000, with $5,000 down. When I sold my interests in 1987, the company had reached $9 billion in annual sales through 450 offices with over eight thousand sales agents.

I started life from very humble beginnings, watching my single mom struggle to make a living as a nanny in London, England, during World War II. After the war, she remarried, and we immigrated to Canada, where I grew up on a remote farm outside Perryvale, near Athabasca in northern Alberta. Although the concept of philanthropy was not instilled in me growing up, I heeded my mother's advice to try to be the best at whatever I decided to do. After a seven-year stint in the Canadian military, I launched my business career and established myself and my family in Victoria, British Columbia. My first charitable experience was for the board of directors of my children's private school in Victoria. Since then, I've enjoyed contributing both time and money to many causes I am passionate about. It has always been clear to me that I could make a difference in the lives of others and my community. However, my quest to help others did not fully solidify until I was struck by tragedy. My life came to an abrupt halt in 2000 when my only son, Todd, who had suffered from a series of mental challenges, committed suicide by jumping from the fourteenth floor of the New York Plaza Hotel. I was devastated, and for the first time was faced with something I could not fix. I continued to exist, but my passion was gone. I had made and lost millions of dollars and had no problem dealing with either. But losing Todd was different. I felt the first true low point of my life. Eventually, I emerged from this state of shock by looking back at my personal system of values-based living. I had a choice: either drown in grief or find myself in my values and can-do attitude and focus all my energy in a positive direction to honor and celebrate Todd's life.

Todd has been our angel. He gives us direction on what to do and where to go. Through the inspiration of Todd's memory; my wife, Rita; and our close friends, I began my mission in two ways. First, we founded the Todd Thomas Foundation in 2000 to celebrate and honor Todd's life, to help raise awareness of mental illness, to address the stigma associated with it, and to support research for effective treatments. We held a fund-raising gala at the Four Seasons Resort in Scottsdale on January 19, 2001, to raise awareness and funds for the foundation, which was established as a component fund of the Arizona Community Foundation in Phoenix.

Second, with the encouragement of a colleague and good friend from the World Presidents' Organization, I decided to galvanize my method of values-based goal setting and share it with others through LifePilot, a British Columbia-based nonprofit organization that provides programs which empower and teach people from all walks of life to live in alignment with their values. I founded LifePilot in 2002 and have since spent countless hours traveling the world with Rita to teach the half-day workshop and touch as many lives with my message as possible. We've grown into an organization with highly qualified navigators and have taught over five thousand individuals ranging from business leaders to students to families to prison inmates.

The passionate entrepreneur in me will never cease to exist, and I've dedicated the past twenty years to an international network organization called Entrepreneurs' Organization, EO. As one of the founding members, and now chairman emeritus, I absolutely love donating my resources and time and sharing my experience and wisdom with young entrepreneurs and our leaders of tomorrow. For the past two years, I've been fortunate to participate as a judge at EO's Global Student Entrepreneur Awards (GSEA) and represent the 2008 judges as chairman of the committee. The 2007 and 2008 competitions in Chicago were among my best days. I have also become a very enthusiastic fan of the Collegiate Entrepreneurs' Organization (CEO), of which I am now the Vice Chairman.

My passion for teaching young individuals and entrepreneurs about the importance of values has presented an opportunity for me to come full circle. In keeping with my message of values-based living and leadership, I collaborated with Royal Roads University in Victoria, British Columbia, to establish the Todd Thomas Institute for Values-Based Leadership. Through the Thomas Foundation, we made a gift in December 2006 to initiate the process. We successfully launched the Institute in July 2008 with a commitment to global leadership for social, environmental, and economic sustainability, and to advance the theory and practice of values-based leadership through applied research with partners in the workplaces and communities.

As an ardent mentor, I always like to leave my readers with the following thoughts: Be individuals of integrity first and foremost, and find balance in your lives. It is critical to identify and keep your core values in front of you at all times (record them in writing) before saying yes to anything so your choices align with your values. Be passionate—be and do your best every single day without exception. Don't ever settle for mediocrity from yourself or others. And lastly, irrespective of the difficulties in life—which will inevitably come your way—never give up, always be positive, and remember: "It's easy; it's a piece of cake!"

Peter H. Thomas

KEY SUCCESS FACTORS: Integrity, Finding Balance in Your Life, Passion, Positive Thinking, Never Giving Up

RECOMMENDED BOOKS: *The Man Who Tapped the Secrets of the Universe* by Glenn Clark, *Think and Grow Rich* by Napoleon Hill, *Blue Ocean Strategy* by W. Chan Kim and Renée Mauborgne, *How to Win Friends and Influence People* by Dale Carnegie

WEB SITE: *www.lifepilot.org*

EDITOR'S NOTES: At age seventy, Peter continues to pursue ways of providing support for the causes he holds dear. He is a role model and values-based leader who has made a major impact both in the business community and in the lives of the many people he has met and touched throughout his illustrious life. An entrepreneur at heart, Peter's life has taken him from serial entrepreneurship to social entrepreneurship, a vocation he will continue to passionately pursue to enrich the lives of others.

KEY SUCCESSES AS SOCIAL ENTREPRENEUR

- Founder and Chairman, LifePilot, *www.lifepilot.org*
- Founder and Chairman, Todd Thomas Institute for Values-Based Leadership at Royal Roads University, *www.royalroads.ca/tti*
- Chairman Emeritus, International Advisory Committee, Entrepreneurs' Organization, *www.eonetwork.org*
- Chairman, 2008 Judges Nominating Committee, Global Student Entrepreneur Awards, *www.gsea.org*
- Vice Chairman, Collegiate Entrepreneurs' Organization, *www.c-e-o.org*

- Chairman, Thomas Foundation, public foundation in Canada focusing on education, children and youth, and mental health
- Chairman, the Todd Thomas Foundation, a component fund of the Arizona Community Foundation focusing on mental health, *www.toddthomasfoundation.org*

PETER'S RULES FOR SUCCESS

1. KISS: Keep it simple simple.
2. Ignore people who say, "It can't be done."
3. Work smart, not hard.
4. Become a student of your chosen career.
5. Be an innovator; study what works and do it better.
6. Emulate the best in your field, but with your own spin.
7. Write down everything, track goals, and follow through daily.
8. Stay focused.
9. Act enthusiastic, and you will be enthusiastic.
10. Be persistent.
11. Practice delegation every day (empower others).
12. Avoid extensive meetings.
13. Make decisions quickly—don't be afraid to make mistakes.
14. Make the most of your day—get up early.
15. Have at least five mentors.
16. Visualize—as Covey said, "Begin with the end in mind."
17. Add an element of fun to all your activities.

It is literally true that you can succeed best and quickest by helping others to succeed.
—*Napoleon Hill*

ENTREPRENEURSHIP IS A TEAM SPORT

My father left the U.S. Air Force in 1961. He had kids and a wife and was returning to his father's home state, looking to buy land for a ranch. He drew a circle with a fifty-mile radius around Tulsa, Oklahoma, and set his eyes on a small spot in the green country just outside of Adair. I came along about nine years after the move—the youngest by a long shot.

Growing up on a ranch, you learn to work. It's expected. We were always at the ranch when not in school or playing sports. There was no time to rest, we never took vacations, and weekends were for catching up on chores we might not have finished during the week.

We raised cattle—a risky business. You're at the mercy of the rain, twisters and hail, commodity prices, and illness. You buy the land, livestock, and supplies you need, hoping you'll manage to make ends meet, or maybe bank a windfall against the next disaster.

Mom and Dad didn't protect us from the harsh realities of ranching. They spoke openly around the kitchen table—letting us know there was work to do, income to earn, and expenses to meet, and that we were an essential part of the team needed to make it happen.

Being the youngest of four, I was motivated by the desire to do what the older kids did. I watched them and learned. Some things I mimicked, some things I avoided. I saw what worked and what didn't and learned to keep my mouth shut and make calculated decisions. At age eight, I began transacting my first bits of business. With Dad's encouragement and under his watchful eye, I bought and sold cattle at auctions, earning myself a nice profit. By the time I was fourteen, I was making deals on my own.

One of the more lucrative deals of my early entrepreneurship involved a neighboring rancher who'd bought a few tractor-trailer loads of watermelons for his livestock. They were almost too ripe to eat but would be viable for consumption for a day or two, and I saw an opportunity. I bargained. If he'd let me sell them, I'd split the profit.

Borrowing Dad's truck, I loaded as many melons as I could and set up shop out on the highway. I cut open a few of the melons to show the ripe, sweet hearts and put up a sign advertising,

"$1 each"—a price I determined by the current value of a good watermelon and the short shelf life of my seemingly endless supply. By the end of the day, enough people had stopped, turned around, and spent a dollar that I'd sold one trailer load. By the end of the third day—and the end of my inventory—I'd sold four hundred melons, paid off my partner, and pocketed $200.

In high school, I played baseball, basketball, and football; ran track; and represented the fifty-eight students of the senior class of Adair High as their president. After graduation, I worked my way through Oklahoma State University by refereeing sports, working summers in chemical and utility plants, and interning at Occidental Petroleum. But long before college and even before high school, I'd learned to recognize opportunity. By discovering the value of honesty, consistency, and keeping things simple, I'd figured out that while home runs are exciting, you need a team of individuals who are willing to work hard and are able to make base hits in order to win the game.

I graduated from OSU in four years—five wasn't an option. With student loans to pay, I had to get out and make a living. The job market for graduates in May of 1992 was tough, even tougher than during the recession of 2008-2009. However, I did find a job, was promoted within six months, and began moving up the career ladder. But I wasn't content. I was born an entrepreneur into a family of entrepreneurs, and I wasn't satisfied sitting in a cubicle or a corner office.

By 1999, I tried something outside of the corporate world with friends in Florida and Atlanta using the nest egg I'd set aside. We had a great idea that's still good, but we were ahead of the game in terms of innovation and wading impatiently through the muck and mire of state government bureaucracy. Before we could turn a profit, the money ran out. I came to Dallas in 2002, closer to home but with no savings. I went to work for an environmental company that owned a number of subsidiaries, including ISNetworld. That's where I met Bill Addy.

ISNetworld, at that time, was an IT development shop and an undeveloped idea. Like many businesses of its kind, it was spread too thin, unprofitable, and needed to be sold. I worked with Bill for about a year before ISNetworld came up for sale. Bill is a brilliant guy with an uncanny ability to absorb and frame strategy, and one of the nicest people you'll ever meet. He and another investor bought the company and worked to reform it for about six months before he called me, saying little more than "I need you." In Bill, I recognized the tenacity, honesty, and dedication I value, and I couldn't wait to come on board.

In 2001, at the age of thirty, I again left corporate life. I resigned from the environmental company, telling the president I was leaving to help retool ISNetworld. He told me, "You're foolish. You're never going to make it." His company went bankrupt and is no longer around, but his words of discouragement motivated me and helped make ISNetworld a success.

Taking over a company in need of a major overhaul is tough and in many ways tougher than starting a business from scratch. Commuting from Dallas to Sugarland, Texas, Bill and I narrowed ISNetworld's broad focus, zeroing in on the low-hanging fruit—the one idea we believed held the greatest potential for success—contractor safety management. We eliminated thirty-two positions from a staff of thirty-five. Bill concentrated on the big picture while I set out to handpick an A-team willing to commit themselves to the cause of creating excellence while working for little more than the promise of a large future reward, if they believed in the team and stayed in the game.

ISNetworld is a service used by contractors and the major oil and gas companies, manufacturing facilities, pharmaceutical companies, and other industrial organizations that depend on those contractors. More than just an online database that manages health and safety data, ISNetworld saves lives, protects communities, and safeguards a company's bottom line.

At the end of 2001, ISNetworld had 50 clients; by the end of 2002, 750. Over the next three years, we added 3,000 clients, and in 2006, practically doubled in size. By concentrating on the capital-intensive petrochemical and pipeline markets, and focusing on companies dependent upon OSHA-compliant subcontractors, ISNetworld has grown at an astronomical rate, fueled by an excellent product and first-rate customer service. As of February 2009, we had 17,500 clients in the United States, Canada, and Australia; and we continue to expand globally.

Plenty of people were ready for us to fail, and it certainly hasn't been easy; but with each barrier, each "you can't" and each "you'll never," our team has proven we can. ISNetworld is becoming the authority in contractor safety management and verification, and those three employees who stayed and all the others who've come on board, trusting us and giving up lucrative positions with guaranteed salaries, are now very successful.

ISNetworld's rapid growth shows no sign of slowing, and this gives me an enormous sense of personal satisfaction. With jobs hard to come by, we're keeping people on staff (while other companies are laying off), recruiting from college campuses, and adding new positions. I have the opportunity to recognize talent and help young men and women achieve the success they dreamed they'd have.

I took a risk eight years ago. It may have seemed foolish to some at the time, but it's been well worth it. Every day I learn something new—from my management team, from our clients, and from the brilliant new hires coming to us right out of school. But no matter what I learn, I remember what I was taught on that ranch outside of Adair, Oklahoma—that success is more attainable and life more satisfying when you work with a dedicated, hardworking, and committed team.

Joe Eastin

KEY SUCCESS FACTORS: Hard Work, Valuing Teamwork, Belief that Money Alone is Not the Reason You Get on the Horse

WEB SITE: *www.isnetworld.com*

EDITOR'S NOTES: Joe Eastin is now President and part owner of ISNetworld, a privately held company. He and his wife, Monica, married in 2004 and live in Dallas, Texas, with their two children. The Eastins are assisting in a long-term effort to revitalize downtown Pryor, the county seat of Mayes County, Oklahoma; and Joe is an active member of the American Cancer Society and founder of WildCatter Literacy.

HOW I LIVE:

- √ Focus on the activity, and do the fundamentals; the money will come.
- √ Be consistent, keep your eye on the ball, and don't add unnecessary complexities.

- √ Be honest—anything gained by the loss of your integrity has no value in the long run. (There's a big difference between an entrepreneur and a wheeler-dealer.)
- √ Don't focus on an exit strategy. Focus on the hit.

Set your goals high and don't stop until you get there.
—Bo Jackson

FROM PASSION AND PERSISTENCE TO PURPOSE AND PROSPERITY

The following story is about an "extreme entrepreneur" partnership presented as His, Hers, and Ours.

His

As a sixteen-year-old sophomore in high school, I decided there was no reason I couldn't be like the dot-com millionaires I read about in magazines. My best friend and I decided to launch a Web design company. We created our very first Web page ever—a Web site announcing our services—and waited for business. The phone rang. We got a meeting. Our company, Princeton WebSolutions, was off to a great start—sort of.

My partner and I had no business experience and were very fearful that, as two high school students, we wouldn't be taken seriously. Furthermore, the meeting was scheduled for the middle of the day (while I was in school) and in a place we needed to be driven (the driving age was seventeen). My friend and I turned our selling skills on our parents, convincing them to let us take a day off from school and to drive us to the meeting. Of course, we needed to be let out a couple blocks away so our potential client wouldn't see us being dropped off by our parents! After nailing every question the client asked, we were awarded our first project for $1,000. From that point, we were in business.

By the time we wound down the company, Princeton WebSolutions had been rated the number one youth-run Web design company in the nation, and I had a number of Entrepreneur of the Year awards under my belt.

Michael Simmons

Hers

At the age of seventeen, I received my acceptance letter to New York University. Growing up in Manchester, New Hampshire, it had been my dream to make my way to the big city in New York. Of course, the annual tuition was more than my parents' income combined, but that was a small obstacle in the face of realizing my big dream. Right?

I applied for scholarship after scholarship, and my mother offered to take out whatever loans necessary to make up the difference. But after months of serious effort, winning scholarships was proving more difficult than I had thought, and finally, I received the worst news of all—due to an inadequate credit score, my mother was not approved for any of the loans.

Scraping together all the money I had saved from afterschool jobs, finding federal loans I could apply for myself, and convincing the university to give me a deferred payment option (so I only had to pay for half of the semester up front), I was on my way. Shortly before classes were to begin, my mother and my grandparents drove me the five hours to New York and dropped me off. I didn't tell them I had used my entire savings to make the first payment and had only $30 left to my name. That wasn't even enough for a bus ticket back home!

I did whatever I could to survive. I used Barnes & Noble gift cards to buy bagel lunches. I stayed in when friends asked me to go out. I smuggled Cheerios from the all-you-can-eat dorm cafeteria. Also, I immediately started working in a public elementary school through a work-study program, making $10 per hour—more than I had ever made, but certainly not on track to get my next college payment submitted. While searching for additional jobs, I worked incredibly hard at the one I had—taking initiative and volunteering to help beyond the call of my job description. But I was running out of options. I was desperate and discouraged, preparing myself to say good-bye to New York. And that's when it happened. After a sleepless night, I made my way to an 8:00 a.m. class and then to the elementary school—where I was offered a $40-an-hour job teaching in an afterschool program. It was unbelievable; I had to keep replaying the conversation in my head to be sure I wasn't crazy.

That piece of luck—created through taking a risk (no one would have come to New Hampshire to offer me the opportunity) and hard work—enabled me to stay through the rest of the semester. I continued to pursue opportunities. By the time I graduated from NYU, I was a senior associate in a venture capital firm hiring and managing people with more experience and education than I had.

Sheena Lindahl

Ours

Our paths crossed at New York University. As we shared our experiences, we began to realize while our challenges were very different, our experiences were very similar. What had made one of us (Michael) successful in business was also enabling the other one (Sheena) to succeed with her college goals. Entrepreneurship in the sense of starting and running a business was very powerful, but so was the entrepreneurial mind-set. This idea of extreme entrepreneurship was a message we knew we had to get out.

We started by taking the ideas we were discussing every night and the information from mentors and successful individuals we were interviewing, and turning them into a book. I (Michael) wrote and organized the content and the result was *The Student Success Manifesto: How to Create a Life of Passion, Purpose, and Prosperity*—which became an Amazon.com best seller.

We started speaking to high school and college students across the country about the concept of extreme entrepreneurship. We found students all over who were doing great things but who felt alone in their ventures. Other students didn't believe it was possible to be successful doing something they loved. In an effort to show it was possible and there were young people out there making great things happen, we brainstormed the idea of the Extreme Entrepreneurship Tour . . . and launched it!

The Extreme Entrepreneurship Tour is the first collegiate entrepreneurship tour to bring top young entrepreneurs to campuses to share their experiences and the lessons they have learned. Rather than hearing about entrepreneurship from people much older than they are, the tour brings the message that they must begin working toward their goals now if they are going to achieve them.

Since its launch, the Extreme Entrepreneurship Tour has held over sixty events in twenty-five states. It has been featured on the AOL home page, as well as appeared on CBS, NBC, and *ABC News* and in *USA Today*. In 2006, we were included in *Business Week*'s list of the country's top twenty-five entrepreneurs under twenty-five. The Extreme Entrepreneurship Tour has received the Innovation Award from the National Association of Development

Organizations and the Program of the Year award from Northern Michigan University.

Of course, the Extreme Entrepreneurship Tour isn't the only way we have partnered. Before becoming business partners, we had a very special relationship. We started dating our third day in New York. Soon after graduation, we were married; and in our greatest venture of all, on November 21, 2008, our daughter, Halle Elyn Simmons, was born. Our family now lives in Plainsboro, New Jersey, where we continue to spread our message of creating a life of passion, purpose, and prosperity.

Michael Simmons and Sheena Lindahl

KEY SUCCESS FACTORS: Focus, Finding Mentors, Passion, Purpose

RECOMMENDED BOOKS: *The E-Myth Revisited* by Michael Gerber, *Good to Great* by Jim Collins, *The Student Success Manifesto* by Michael Simmons

WEB SITE: *www.extremetour.org, www.journeypage.com*

EDITOR'S NOTES: Michael Simmons and Sheena Lindahl have been keynote speakers on the topics of student success and youth entrepreneurship at events and conferences from Washington State to Washington DC. As 2005 graduates of New York University, authors, teachers, speakers, and award-winning entrepreneurs, they are able to deliver a unique perspective that connects with audiences. Recently, Michael and Sheena were named by *Business Week* as one of the country's top twenty-five entrepreneurs under twenty-five. Michael has been the winner of three Entrepreneur of the Year awards from the National Foundation for Teaching Entrepreneurship, Fleet, and the National Coalition for Empowering Youth Entrepreneurship. Michael and Sheena have just launched *The Virtual Incubator,* providing students with a system to take action every day toward starting a business.

What lies behind us and what lies before us are small matters compared to what lies within us.
　　　　　　　　　　　　—Ralph Waldo Emerson

CHANCE: GOLF GAME AND A TORNADO

Semitrailers? I hardly knew the difference between a reefer and a dry van. When I graduated from Claremore High School and went to Oklahoma State University, I chose Accounting as a major because I knew I'd be able to use it to get a good job. I had no idea what I really wanted to do except to make good money to take care of the family I hoped to have.

I pretty much put myself through college. I had good summer jobs and also worked during school. My mom helped here and there with spending money but didn't tell my dad.

While a junior, I was able to intern at the prestigious firm of Price Waterhouse. This internship was continued in my senior year, and after graduating with a degree in accounting/finance, I became a full-time accountant at the firm. Later, I moved to Coopers & Lybrand in Tulsa. I was seemingly successful in the corporate world, but without a sense of fulfillment. I was good at my job but needed a challenge. Thankfully, it fell onto my lap in the form of a golf game.

One of the partners at Coopers was scheduled to play golf with a guy but couldn't make it, so I played in his place. The "guy" was Ronnie Jett, owner of Utility Tri-State in Tulsa. During the game, I happened to ask Ronnie if any of his rich friends needed someone to run their business because I had grown weary of tax accounting. Jett suggested I come to Utility and run it. Jett's company became a customer of Coopers & Lybrand, and for the next eighteen months, I conducted Utility's audits and prepared tax returns, all the while gaining an understanding of the company's financial situation.

It wasn't a pleasant situation. The industry was in the doldrums, and Utility was struggling to find a measure of stability. The company had a negative net worth, and it was time to get this trailer on the road.

Becoming vice president of Utility Tri-State was not glamorous at all. I gave up a comfortable job for $600 a month and 49 percent of the business—at a company with a negative net worth. I did, luckily, have a safety net, but didn't ever plan on using it. Coopers told me if this didn't work out, I was always welcome to come back; but I was determined not to admit failure. We survived because of my wife's job.

Jett and I worked long hours. As vice president, most of my time was spent doing financials and making the facility's five acres look presentable, both inside and out. In the nine months prior to my arrival, Utility had not sold one new trailer. I could see what we needed to do: sales were going to be critical for this business to survive, and parts and service needed to grow as well.

I took an active role, which continues to this day, in trailer sales and hired good people to manage and grow the parts and service departments. Within three months, we had sold fifty flatbeds—and our parts and service departments had made $357!

I still wasn't able to take home any money, and I admitted to my wife that I might have made a mistake. It had been the best month in a long time, but there was still no profit.

But I didn't give up. I went into overdrive, and finally the parts and service department became profitable. I made working fun, and after a time, it no longer seemed like work. I got to know my customers and developed great working relationships with them.

And then, one year later, Utility Tri-State was flattened. In the heart of tornado alley, on April 24, 1993, almost one year to the day that I joined the company, a devastating storm, bearing winds of 250 miles per hour, leveled our facility before jumping across I-44. This storm killed seven and injured about one hundred people in the Tulsa area. No one was in our facility at the time; I had left at about 4:30 p.m., planning to return about 8:00 p.m. to meet a customer who was picking up a trailer.

Nothing except one metal file box, which we still use today, was saved from the tornado. Total, gut-wrenching devastation.

Jett and I had business interruption insurance, and within ninety days, we were back. Smaller and with fewer employees, but we were back. This industry is capital intensive, and I think the tornado blew the fire out of Jett. I wanted to take the company in a different direction and convinced him to sell me his 51 percent share, making me sole owner of Utility Tri-State. Jett remains a close friend to this day, and I am forever grateful to him.

This was the first day of the rest of Utility's life. I began to move the business forward, and by the end of 1994, I had tripled the company's revenue in trailer sales over the previous year—from $2.7 million to $8.6 million—and doubled its net income. By 1997, trailer sales had grown to $23.6 million, and in 1998, to $31.5 million.

I also created a working atmosphere with the employees in mind. To improve the working conditions in the service area, I started by moving a noisy compressor so the employees could communicate, and then installed air lines around the entire shop to provide air pressure for tools.

The yard was in desperate need of a cleanup. Five years' worth of junk had accumulated, so I organized a voluntary cleanup project. I wanted employees to be proud of where they worked, as well as for the customers to feel comfortable when they drove into our yard. I wanted it to look like a successful business.

I couldn't afford to pay my people for their cleanup work, but I promised to feed them well, and I did. I had dinner delivered by one of the best barbecue houses in Tulsa, a tradition that continues today. We often grill in the summer, or someone will cook and bring food to work. Gathering for a meal brings us together like a family.

I also started providing benefits—uniforms, health insurance, paid vacations, and a quarterly bonus program. Additionally, I added a payroll-deduction retirement plan that includes an employer contribution at the end of the year. I wanted my people to feel a sense of ownership to give them an incentive to grow the business with me.

Employees need to understand we care about them. I want my employees to know they are all important no matter what their position within the company. I encourage innovation, and as a result, Utility Tri-State has been instrumental in developing new flooring systems for refrigerated trailers. This sense of caring needs to flow over into customers, as well as into employees. I take existing as well as new customers to our factories to see how their trailers are built. The customer is involved in discussions with plant management as well as with corporate staff.

With business taking off in Tulsa, it was time to expand. In 1995, in a one-room portable building and three trailers, I hired a salesman I had known in college; and we set up a sales facility east of Fort Smith in Alma, Arkansas. Today, after an investment of over $1 million, it is a state-of-the-art facility, including a sixty-foot paint booth, with about thirty employees.

In 1998, the expansion came to include Oklahoma City. This location is still growing, but for now employs only eleven, and has recently moved to a larger facility to accommodate its growing customer base.

Today, we are fighting the economy just as the rest of America. Luckily, our industry, while hit hard, is one that will remain. Consumer goods must move, and trucking is the most popular way, at present, to move them.

Jeff Smith

KEY SUCCESS FACTORS: Passion, Competitiveness, Work Ethic, Perseverance

RECOMMENDED BOOKS: Books by Harvey Mackay and his daily column at www.timesunion.com and books by Norman Vincent Peale

EDITOR'S NOTES: Jeff Smith, the President and owner of Utility Tri-State, is married and has four children. Jeff enjoys golf, going to Grand Lake with his family, and Oklahoma State University athletics.

Learn to smile at every situation. See it as an opportunity to prove your strength and ability.
—*Joe Brown*

LIFE STRATEGIST

On October 1, 2005, I attended a barbecue at a friend's house, and in my usual social fashion, I mingled equally with people I knew and people I hadn't met. One of my new acquaintances was Suzanne—a wiry, energetic, outspoken blonde. I explained to her that I intended to move back to Chicago in a couple of weeks because I hadn't been able to find full-time employment in Des Moines after resigning from my previous job. I had kept busy over the previous month with looking for employment and doing freelance journalism work that came to me through my professional contacts. But I wanted to hop back on the corporate track ASAP.

Suzanne leaned toward me with one hand on her hip and her eyes twinkling and said, "Elizabeth, you love what you're doing. And it's working! Why don't you go for it?"

My head tilted to the side; I gave her a quizzical look. *Who, me?* I thought. *Be an entrepreneur? Isn't that risky?* But after thinking it over for a couple of days, I decided Suzanne was right and so began my entrepreneurial adventure.

Prior to this encounter, I had my heart set on advancing in the corporate world. But after more than three years as a full-time entrepreneur with Grace Communications Inc. (where I write magazine articles, marketing materials, and books) and Real Life E® (where I do speaking, training, and coaching for women in business), I've never been happier.

My business required rapid learning. I hadn't studied entrepreneurship, let alone planned to start a business one year out of college. That meant I had to figure out all of my legal and accounting systems as I went. (I recommend doing this in advance whenever possible—it was messy sorting everything out once I had already started the business.) Also, along the way, I needed to work on defining what services I provided and what I was worth.

During the first nine months, I was incredibly fortunate to have an almost-constant stream of work from my journalism contacts throughout the United States. (I studied magazine journalism in college, completed four internships, and worked for magazines full-time before venturing out on my own.) To keep my sanity and grow a sustainable business, I learned I needed to say no to lower-paying projects, like doing basic research, and focus on higher-value work like writing, editing, and photo styling.

About one year into Grace Communications Inc., I went from being so busy that I needed to turn down or subcontract work to not having any projects. This was the fall of 2006, and huge changes were hitting the print publishing industry. If I didn't expand my client base, I was going out of business. Throughout my second year, I focused on writing services but expanded my target market from national magazines to local magazines, marketing materials, and books. This strategy allowed me to continue as an entrepreneur despite the changes in my market.

In the summer of 2007, I decided to make an even bigger change and to develop a new business that could enable me to inspire others and to build a scalable company. After working with a business coach, I settled on the idea of pursuing a speaking, training, and coaching business; and Real Life E® was born.

I am rapidly moving through my fourth year and am excited to have more opportunities to encourage women to pursue their dreams through my new business. Real Life E® focuses on "time strategies to create a brilliant life in a burnt-out world" by offering training, speaking, and coaching on how to organize your life and your schedule. I look forward to expanding my business into products like books and audio downloads and growing it to build job opportunities for others. But most of all, I am excited to see women achieve work-and-life balance (I personally aim to work forty hours a week) so they can excel inside and outside of work.

As this story shows, one of the biggest keys to my longevity is my ability to adapt by learning new skills and serving new markets. Instead of fearing change, I've embraced it. One of my mottos throughout my entrepreneurial journey is "You're not entitled to success." If something is no longer working, I need to do something different.

Another key element to the growth of my businesses, especially Real Life E®, is moving beyond networking to true partnering with other people. Through participating in the Extreme Entrepreneurship Tour in the fall of 2008, I gained so much from sharing ideas and collaborating with other young entrepreneurs. During this time, I also developed a support network, including two other young female entrepreneurs that I talk with on a weekly basis and an older mentor whom I consult monthly.

I never expected to become an entrepreneur, but I have so enjoyed the journey. By being open to change and to the people around me, I've experienced and accomplished more in three years than most people do in thirty.

Elizabeth Grace Saunders

KEY SUCCESS FACTORS: Adaptability, Collaboration

RECOMMENDED BOOKS: *Getting Things Done* by David Allen

WEB SITE AND BLOG: *www.RealLifeE.com*

EDITOR'S NOTES: Elizabeth's writing has appeared in over forty-five different publications, and she has spoken to more than a thousand individuals in ten states. When she's not traveling, Elizabeth enjoys spending time with family and friends, exploring the outdoors, and growing deeper in her faith.

You can't measure the heart of a champion.
—Anonymous

THE FOOT DOCTOR

It all started when I got cut from my last National Football League (NFL) team. I had been bouncing around the NFL after finishing football at New Mexico State University in Las Cruces, New Mexico, in 1982. But after five years of trying to fulfill my dream of being an NFL punter, I decided it was time to turn the page and start a new chapter of my life. I knew if I had to finish college and get a job, I wanted it to be related to football. Besides construction work, football was what I had done my entire life, and it was really what I loved the most.

After graduation, I chose to go back home to Ruidoso, New Mexico, to try to get a job at my old high school. I ended up coaching the defensive ends, offensive backs, and special teams for the varsity team. As a side job, I began to give kicking lessons. Although I was making money, this wasn't the way I wanted to work for the rest of my life. I had heard of Ben Agajanian, the kicking coach for the Dallas Cowboys throughout the Tom Landry era in Dallas, Texas. He ran kicking and punting camps in the summers and developed some of the premier kickers and punters in college and the NFL.

Growing up, I had always thought about doing something similar but never really thought I could make enough money or have the name recognition to make a living. However, Ben Agajanian was doing very well for himself—maybe I could do it too.

I had success as a football coach at my former high school in Ruidoso and coached the unanimous two-way, first team all-state kicker and punter. At that time, Eastern New Mexico University brought me on as a defensive ends coach; and as I was a formidable kicking coach, by default, I was in charge of the kickers and punters. Over the next two years, both the kicker and punter became first Team Kodak All-Americans.

In 1989, I seized the opportunity to move to Dallas, where I became the assistant head football coach, defensive backs coach, and special teams coordinator at Bishop Lynch High School. In 1990, a friend of mine who had been to the Ben Agajanian Kicking Camps suggested I go meet him. We had instant rapport. He offered me a job running his camps, and I quickly accepted. At that moment, I knew I would have my chance to do what I had always dreamed of doing—kicking a football and making money doing it (even if it was not me doing the kicking). Of course, running these camps didn't immediately bring in enough money to achieve my goal of running my own kicking business. Since Ben lived in the Los Angeles area, I even tried to run some kicking camps of my own, but the client base was lacking—and I still didn't have a reputation or a name.

Being a football coach, I had minimal structure in the business sense, and the hours invested coaching Texas high school football were staggering! But the foundation and the passion to create the best kickers and punters in the country were laid—I was hooked.

I knew how to kick and punt a football, and I could do it very well. But I needed a larger client base. Because I was a good teacher, I also knew I needed to develop drills and techniques that would help players go beyond anything anyone else was teaching.

I continued to run the Ben Agajanian Kicking Camps from 1991 to 1999. During that time, in 1994, I took a coaching position at Garland High School in Texas, and ran the camps for Ben in the summers. Both programs achieved excellence during those years, and it was an exciting opportunity for me to develop my coaching abilities and to mentor kids who loved the sport to which I had devoted my life's dream.

In 1997, I quit the teaching business and became partners with a former kicker from Miami. We tried to take Ben's camps to another level, but soon my partner decided to move on. We gave the camps back to Ben, and my kicking business in the Dallas area started to slowly fade away. As I looked for other opportunities in other business avenues, the anger set in. I was fed up with this kicking business and told God I would never coach again.

Well, as fate would have it, three days after that quote, the University of Texas called and asked me to run their kicking camp in the summer of 1999—so I did. My passion and desire for excellence was hotter than ever before—defeat once again opened a door to greater opportunity.

After that summer, I went back to coach at Garland High School. On the side, I gave kicking lessons to ten to fifteen kickers and punters from Ben's camps and others I had met through the University of Texas. I did private lessons and camps during the fall and spring or whenever I had a free moment during the weekends from coaching.

I used some of the drills and techniques Ben taught me; however, through my knowledge of kinesiology and biomechanics, I continued to develop new successful techniques of my own. Over the next year, the business grew exponentially.

Other colleges such as SMU (Southern Methodist University) and the University of Houston hired me to run their kicking camps. Before long, I had more lessons than time allowed, and I was still holding down a full-time teaching and coaching position. In the summer of 2000, at one of my private camps, there were college kickers and punters representing the whole Big 12 South and numerous others from many other conferences—I had to be doing something right!

In December of 2001, I quit coaching football to be a full-time kicking and punting coach and consultant. I was not sure what to expect, and business did not boom right away. I worked with five to ten athletes on a weekly basis, and when I put on a one-day or two-day camp, as many as twenty-five guys might show up. It was hard at first because business was not steady. If parents or athletes didn't call or come to my camps, I wasn't making money. Also, the students with whom I worked were getting older and moving on to college to kick or were just not kicking anymore. I kept praying and thinking of different ways to attract new kids. I went to local high schools and coaching clinics and talked to the coaches. I sent out brochures to all the schools. But what set me apart from others attempting to do something similar was the success ratio of the kickers and punters with whom I worked. Names such as Guru and The Best started to echo throughout Texas and the Southwest.

Word spread and I was invited to speak at several coaching clinics. Schools would bring me in to clinic their coaches. Athletes started flying in to Dallas, or parents would bring me into their cities to teach their sons how to kick a football. After about two years, I realized I had coached more than two hundred athletes on a personal basis, including high school, college, and professionals.

As the result of years of perseverance, dedication, a passion for kicking, and working as hard as I possibly could, I have now built my business to work with thousands of athletes across the country.

Camps have expanded to include Dallas, Houston, Lubbock, and Austin, Texas, as well as Louisiana, Oklahoma, South Carolina, Kentucky, and Alabama. I have worked with kickers and punters from the West Coast to the East Coast, from Canada to Mexico, and everywhere in between. I represent kickers and punters from the NFL, Big 12, the Southeastern Conference (SEC), Conference USA, Mountain West, and numerous other divisions from D-I to NAIA.

Today, I look forward to football season, as I can humbly watch high school, college, and professional football and see my boys playing in almost every venue. Without prayer and faith, hard work, perseverance, and the "don't give up" attitude, there is no way I would be where I am today.

Rocky Willingham
Contributed by Matt Fodge

KEY SUCCESS FACTORS: Faith, Passion, Perseverance, Work Ethic

WEB SITE: *www.RWKSKicking.com*

EDITOR'S NOTES: Rocky Willingham is known as the best kicking coach in the country. RWKS now serves as a consultant to over fifty colleges and universities and runs camps for twenty D-I universities, eight of which are in the top twenty-five. RWKS has had multiple All-Americans, over twenty All-Conference kickers, fifty-plus high school All-State Kickers/Punters, several Lou Groza Award finalists, and three Ray Guy Award winners. One of Rocky's students, and the contributor of this story, Matt Fodge, is a punter for Oklahoma State University and recently was awarded the prestigious Ray Guy Award, the highest achievement for collegiate punters.

CHAPTER TWO

LIVING THE DREAM

Go confidently in the direction of your dreams. Live the life you have imagined.
—Henry David Thoreau

Follow your heart and your dreams will come true.
—Anonymous

ALIVE AND WELL AND LIVIN' THE DREAM

As awesome as it was to have girls screaming, screaming as if they were on fire as I performed on stage, it was never what held my interest for music. Music was my passion. It made me feel special and unique. The blanket of love and support around me eventually boosted my confidence and inspired me to take a chance on the music industry as a career.

When I was young, my grandfather was hospitalized for triple bypass surgery. At that time, there was a high degree of concern something might go wrong during such a procedure. My grandfather and I always had a strong bond, and this surgery made me realize life is short.

As my grandfather recovered, we began paying more attention to music. At first it was just an old guitar in his bedroom closet. I always managed to make my way back there to suggest we get it out. He knew three chords, kind of—enough to play most of the songs he knew. His music heroes became mine. My parents began to notice my genuine excitement for music, and years of lessons and teachers followed. I hated the lessons and could not believe my own loving mother would let these freaky people take me in a room and shut the door. On top of that, I was still young, and my hands were small. I couldn't play chords, so I had to learn to read music from books. "Oh boy, next week I get to learn to play 'She'll Be Coming Around the Mountain'." Even though practice was something I avoided at all cost, on Saturdays my dad would ask me to entertain him while he worked in the garage. I had never seen a man so overwhelmed and in awe of those stale, boring Mel Bay guitar lesson songs. After skipping around to several teachers over the years, I finally found someone who bothered to ask me, "What kind of music do you like?" When I answered, he told me to bring him a record and he would teach me how to play that kind of music. He changed my life. He could listen to music and learn to play it, and within two lessons, he had taught me to do the same. From that day forward, the boundaries between loving music and actually being able to play it seemed to vanish.

Teachers at school began to notice, and I played in talent shows starting in sixth grade. By junior high, I was in an actual band; and in high school, I got the nerve to sing out loud. My friends noticed, and it became the norm for guitar pulls to occur whenever there was a gathering. My best friend at the time was planning on going to Oklahoma State University. I had been so wrapped up in music that I really hadn't given college much thought, but it seemed simple enough to jump on the OSU bandwagon, so I did.

My friend's dad had been a frat boy, and he planned to follow in his footsteps. Since I was following my friend, I jumped on that bandwagon too—for about two weeks. Did you know the general plan is to torture the pledges? I didn't. They put us all in a bunkhouse-style room with assigned beds. They assigned me a bottom bunk. My bunkmate, the guy above me, was more than just a portly fellow and it got worse. On the first night, he stood in front of me as I lay in my bed. "I love to sleep naked," he said as he peeled his underwear off and climbed up to his bunk. I knew how to weld and wished I could lay a few more beads on the rickety pipes which held that big naked man over my head. I don't remember sleeping that night, or any of the next ones. After about two weeks, I de-pledged, realizing there are such things as irreconcilable differences.

The campus had no place to put me, so I moved into a commons area at Bennett Hall while they looked for free space. Room 402 opened up at Iba Hall, a nice room that was mine—mine alone, with not even a roommate. But being alone when you're already a loner is not necessarily a good thing, and I began to get bored. After hearing about an open mike night in the student union, I approached Jamie, the young lady who ran the show. With guitar in hand, I asked if I could sing a song or two. They all made me feel very welcome.

I sang three songs, showed my appreciation to the listeners, and then put up my guitar and sat in the crowd. People were kind with compliments, but one person went farther; he told me of a friend he thought I should contact. I took the number but really had no plans to call. After a couple more weeks, I dialed the number. A chipper voice answered, and I could hear music in the background. The voice simply said, "Hey pal, come on down and pick with us." Two flights down in the same building, I knocked on room 202. Garth Brooks answered the door. I walked into that room a loner, but left enlightened—with new friends and a fresh hope for music.

We played for several hours, each taking turns picking and singing. Garth had an old cassette recorder that we set on the floor between us, and we made our first recording that day. Garth sang "Rocky Top," and I sang "Listen to the Radio." I was so excited! When I got back to my room, I called my parents and told them about my afternoon. The following weekend, I took the tape home and proudly presented it to them. My mom looked at me and asked, "Now what was the other boy's name who was singing with you?" Heck, I wasn't sure, but I thought his name was Garf or something like that, so my mom wrote "Ty and Garf" on the cover of the cassette tape. I wish I had that tape today.

Garth and I would play anywhere, from the library steps to the Bennet Hall lunchroom. We just wanted to make music. When Garth left for Nashville, we made the "Pact." Garth: "Pal, if I ever make it in the music business, I will want you to be there." Of course, I replied, "Well, if I ever make it, I would want you to be there too."

Garth called me the day he signed his deal. I had just finished my degree, had a full-time job, and was being offered a management position with a company. The road split right in front of me. As much as I always wanted to believe I could make it in the music business, I never really had the confidence to take the risk. But I knew Garth had it, whatever *it* was. Although I told Garth to let me think about it for a few days, the fact is I gave notice the next morning and moved to Nashville within the month.

It was hard at first. I took a day job, and we rehearsed at night. The pay was low. Often it was pizza and a lot of promises. Then came the Spam Jam; yes, the canned meat. It was our first real full-band gig. I could barely make my fingers move on the neck of my guitar. Without a doubt, it was a weak performance. Garth skyrocketed into stardom. There were a lot of tests and trials behind the scenes on our way toward the peak, but to the audience, it seemed we were riding high from the start.

After a few years, Nashville labels came calling and this time, they were dialing my number. Now was the chance to chase my own dreams. Garth had let me become such an integral part of his stage show that it was not the most comfortable situation. During a trip overseas, we decided it was time, and I signed with RCA records in 1994. Garth went on to Australia, and I came home to make *Ty England*, my first Nashville recording. Thankfully, it included a hit called "Shoulda Asked Her Faster."

Things were very different by then thanks to Garth's success. Country music had exploded and the year I signed a record deal, there were more than one hundred new acts. The glut of new music being delivered to radio made it very difficult to rise to the top. After another album and five more singles, RCA let me go. In a tailspin, I moved my family back home to Oklahoma. It wasn't long before Capitol Records picked up where RCA left off. Garth and I made an album together for the first time, and it was everything I had hoped it would be. After spending several years apart, I enjoyed the year we spent together and was very proud of the album and the sounds it delivered. Capitol, however, was in turmoil. A new president appeared two months before my album was complete. I personally delivered a rough copy to him; and then I waited two months. Finally, I called to ask what he thought of the new music. He replied, "I'm sorry, but I haven't had time to listen to it yet." When I told Garth about the conversation, he requested a group meeting with the label. I left that meeting having lost yet another record deal. Too country was the verdict. Everyone was going pop.

I was emotionally devastated. I applied for jobs and interviewed with three major pharmaceutical corporations. Each time, I made it all the way to the short list of two. Each time, the company flew me and the other somebody somewhere for the final grilling. Each time, they called me in first. Each time, they explained how much they thought of me. Each time, they told me that their job was beneath me and expressed their fear I would not stay long enough for them to recover their investment in me.

I didn't know what to do. After scraping by for another year, one afternoon, I listened to my last CD and wondered how I might put myself back to work. I had some business cards printed using my first name (Gary) and started calling fairs and festivals selling my own shows as if I were my agent. I learned how to use Adobe Photoshop to create my own promotional materials and mailed them out relentlessly. I tried out band members and put my first Oklahoma-based band together. It was hard work, but eventually, I found some great players. Venues started responding to my promotion efforts, and soon I was writing my own contracts for future shows. The year 2003 was admittedly a light year, but 2004 picked up considerably. In 2005, I met some other musicians, and we started our own record label. After several writing sessions, we cut our first album called *Alive and Well and Livin' the Dream* on Triple T Records. The album title was my statement to those who had so let me down in the music industry. I had been knocked down, but knew I was capable. After all, it is my passion; and I still believe if you want it badly enough, you can find a way to have it. Whatever *it* is.

Ty England

KEY SUCCESS FACTORS: Desire, Endurance, Faith, Willingness to Suffer and Sacrifice for the Cause

RECOMMENDED BOOKS: The Bible

WEB SITES: *www.tyengland.com,*
www.myspace/tyenglandaliveandwell

EDITOR'S NOTE: Ty England lives near Oklahoma City and is usually involved with his greatest passion of all—Aspen, Tyler, Levi, and Matt—hopefully, all future Cowboys!

The past cannot be changed. The future is yet in your power.

—*Hugh White*

STAYING POWER

As a woman, I have always believed that *staying power* for an entrepreneur is the power to withstand many obstacles. I believe every decision is a growing experience, and I never regret any mistake but try to learn from it.

My chapter begins in Iran, where I grew up during the Shah administration with my parents and seven brothers and sisters. My parents were well educated and taught me about different religions, cultures, and nationalities. Prior to the revolution in 1979, when the Ayatollah Khomeini regime was established in Iran, women had more freedom and did not have to follow the Muslim religion. Women had as much freedom as women in America, except they could not vote.

I was married by proxy in Iran and began a new chapter in my life when we moved to the States for his education. My dream of starting a new life in the United States because of the education, culture, and freedom I had read about in magazines and newspapers was becoming a reality.

My challenge with living in America was facing many obstacles to freedom and success. Early in my career, I faced immense challenges in the business world due to being a woman. After working my way up from billing clerk to top salesperson in a transportation company, I was in line for the position of vice president. Unfortunately for me, the president of the company was less than supportive of my application for the opening. He sent me a letter saying the company would hire a woman vice president "over my dead body!"

I was not deterred by my boss's declaration, but rather, I used it as incentive to become an entrepreneur. With my determination and skills, I ultimately broke through the gender barrier and launched a successful global company, Kayhan International. A multiservice organization, Kayhan International, specializes in adaptable design, contract furniture, installation, relocation, and refurbishment of office furniture. It was my answer to the rejection I faced while trying to ascend the corporate ladder.

I knew the only way to be successful was to work for myself. I took a job at a furniture company for a few months before taking a year off to do market research. Knowing I had the skills and knowledge to start my own company, I put together my business plan.

My plan was a bit unorthodox—I hired people who were just beginning their careers and had never worked in the furniture industry. I wanted fresh blood so I could train them myself. Many of the employees who were there when the company was founded are still with the company after twenty-five years. I attribute this loyalty to the strong bonds I have formed with everyone who works for me—a practice I believe is a trademark of women-owned businesses. I also believe in flexibility within the workplace so employees never have to choose between work and family.

There were three major obstacles or challenges in my life and my career, and I credit my values and upbringing for being able to overcome them.

1. The challenge of establishing a woman-owned business competing in a male-dominated industry. There were few female entrepreneurs at the time, but I knew I could pursue my passion and overcome this obstacle to build a very successful business.
2. The financial aspect—being able to save money with my husband and not borrow from any financial institution. The concern was whether we had the financial strength to work with just our own money.
3. The political and economic climate of the '80s and whether it would interfere with the operation of my business. Jimmy Carter was president when I started my company, and interest rates were 22 percent!

Along with building strong relationships, I know good service plays an important role in the success of any business. I make sure more than one person in the company, including me, knows each of our clients and takes a personal interest in their work and personal lives. Using a team approach, as opposed to a commission-based strategy, ensures our clients feel important, reassured, and a part of the Kayhan family.

The foundation of my company is based on:

1. BUILDING LONG-TERM RELATIONSHIPS
   I have always sought to build long-term partnerships with clients rather than simply sell contract furniture. It is this philosophy that inspires me to always look for a better, more cost-effective way to do business that can have a positive impact on clients. Every project is approached with directness and honesty. My customers understand that the Hellriegel team works in their best interest. Part of being a quality supplier is being a good listener. Because of our commitment to strong communication, our clients have come to realize that Hellriegel International will do whatever is humanly and technologically possible to communicate effectively and meet their requirements.

2. INVESTING IN THE FUTURE
   Anticipating the needs of my customers and staying ahead of technology trends helps to maintain a leadership role in the industry. With sound, strategic planning and a corporate philosophy of growth through quality service, I invest in my staff and in the company's operations. I view responding to change as both a challenge and an opportunity. Through continuous improvement and a constant focus on the future, I strive to be the number one provider of quality office systems and office furnishings.

3. DEDICATED PEOPLE
   No company can implement a quality program without a talented and dedicated staff solidly committed to customer satisfaction and firmly rooted on the principles of the team approach to problem solving. I proudly stand behind this philosophy. We have a team of architects, interior designers, sales representatives, marketing personnel, and administrative staff who are all willing to put in the effort to solve problems and achieve positive results. Our staff is encouraged to make decisions and take responsibility at every level. A hands-on approach from concept to completion is irreplaceable.

4. CUSTOMER SATISFACTION

My philosophy is to bring a new dimension of unyielding commitment to better myself and my staff so that Kayhan International's clients benefit. I attribute the successful completion of hundreds of facilities around the world to my pledge of creating environments that enhance the workplace. With this, customer referral has always been a consistent source of business for the company. I am proud to be associated with distinguished organizations both here and abroad that reflect superior achievement in their individual areas. New opportunities are welcomed and I rise to the challenge of bringing collaborative ideas to those who surround me.

Kayhan Hellriegel

KEY SUCCESS FACTORS: Customer Service, Relationships, Dedicated Staff

WEB SITE: *www.kayhan.com*

EDITOR'S NOTES: Kayhan Hellriegel is a proud wife, mother, and grandmother of two. She is now married to Dan Hellriegel.

Kayhan Hellriegel is a founding member of Workplace Alliance network—an innovative network of Haworth Preferred Dealers with a common vision to provide their clients with the most creative, cost-effective, and flexible workplace solutions wherever they do business. She is also a founding member of CREW (Chicago Real Estate Executive Women). It is the preeminent organization for senior-level executive women in the Chicago real estate industry.

For the past ten years, Kayhan Hellriegel has been the honorary chair for the annual Chicago Commercial Real Estate Awards. This event is often referred to as the Oscars of the Chicago commercial real estate industry. The proceeds from this benefit go to the Greater Chicago Food Depository. In 2007, the event raised over $1 million, which allowed the Greater Chicago Food Depository to purchase over 4 million meals for Chicago's hungry.

In March of 2008, for the second straight year, the event raised over $1 million.

In 2007, Hellriegel was chairperson for the East West University Fund Raiser Scholarship Dinner. Through Hellriegel's leadership, attendance increased 40 percent; and for the first time, the event raised more than $100,000. Because of the success of the 2007 event, Hellriegel was asked to be the chairperson again for the November 2008 Scholarship Dinner.

In partnership with the U.S. State Department, Women Impacting Public Policies (WIPP), U.S. Afghan Women's Council, and Northwood University, twelve Afghan women business owners were invited to visit the United States to engage in a high-level business training and mentoring in late August 2007. Hellriegel was honored by being asked to host and mentor three of the Afghan businesswomen for one week. At the end of their visit, Hellriegel was invited to attend a special ceremony at the White House to honor these Afghan women.

If you can DREAM it, you can do it.

—*Walt Disney*

LIVING THE AMERICAN DREAM

Born in 1958 in the mountains of Lebanon, I grew up and attended high school in a war-torn country. My future in Lebanon after high school looked hopeless. With relatives in the USA, I was encouraged by many people to move to the United States to continue my education and make a future for myself and my family. So I left Lebanon in 1979 as a newlywed and moved to the USA with my wife.

My first stop was New York City, where I spent a few short months. Although exciting, New York City proved to be for the more experienced, so I moved to Oklahoma in 1980 to attend Oklahoma State University. Having been raised in the mountains, nature had always been my love and interest. From a young age, my dream was to one day have my own orchard. This passion led me to the Horticulture Department at OSU. With the responsibility of supporting a family in Tulsa, I commuted daily from Stillwater to Tulsa while working three jobs. Graduating in 1984 with a Bachelor of Science in Horticulture, I then proceeded to work in the field I loved so much by starting a lawn-care business, specializing in spraying and exterminating. Unfortunately, asthma did not allow me to last long in that field, so I moved to the business world as a franchise owner and operator of Garfield's restaurant. My free spirit and entrepreneurial thinking did not allow me to be bound by the franchise's rules and regulations. I changed the menu, the hours of operation, the employees' salaries, and the restaurant's decor. The restaurant was performing better than most others in the area, which prompted a visit from headquarters. Oops! I heard words that I did not want to hear: "Mr. Nasreddine, you cannot change the menu, you cannot change the hours, and you cannot change anything since you bought into a franchise." Like a bird in a cage, I was not free to fly. I moved on to manage another restaurant, where I also made incredible improvement. During my restaurant days, I was the victim of an armed robbery and assault. Again, being a free-spirited thinker, I tried to negotiate with the robber, telling him maybe he should find a new career, and that he could actually do better if he had a job. With a broken jaw wired shut for months, along with many cuts and bruises, I learned lesson one in negotiations: never try to negotiate with an armed criminal.

Because of the injuries, I was unemployed for a period of time. Then my friend convinced me to work with him at Golden Buffalo Fine Jewelry. I had worked with a gold dealer in Lebanon, but not with anything like diamonds. Quickly, I gained the knowledge required, and being a thinker rather than a follower, I approached my employer one day with a novel idea. Why not charge less and sell more? Why not build a business based on volume and market domination instead of greed and enormous profit margins? Unwilling to listen, my employer laughed at me and told me how naïve and inexperienced I was. "That is not how the business world works. Son, that's not how we do it here!"

I was convinced there was a better way to do business, so I left Buffalo Fine Jewelry and started Jewelry Replacement Services in 1990 while working side jobs to help support my family and my newborn venture. Using the phonebook, I contacted all the insurance agents in the area, mailing out letters and price lists and offering to help them settle their jewelry claims at wholesale prices. I was elated if I got one response from the thousands of letters mailed. My inventory was a catalog, a box, and a price list backed by my determination and vision for the future. I drove across town many times to deliver a $90 gold band and went above and beyond to please and build a clientele. My car insurance rates went sky high because of all the accidents I had trying to deliver those bands on time to make a $10 profit! That's when the deliveries stopped.

My business grew literally one person at a time. My thought was, *If I can provide this service to insurance companies, why not the public?* With a two-line ad in the classifieds, I worked by appointments from a small office in Tulsa. In order to find me, you had to know someone who knew someone who knew me. My referral business grew day after day, and so did my dedication to this idea. No longer just a replacement service for insurance companies, Jewelry Replacement Services became Israel Diamond Supply in 1995. My idea of providing a diamond at the same cost a jeweler is able to acquire it was producing incredible results. My belief in what I was doing grew deeper every day, especially when reading the letters from the happy and grateful couples whose dreams were realized, without having to pay off the mortgage and the ring at the same time. The competition started taking notice of the "new guy in town." Israel Diamond Supply was suddenly the intruder, who, according to the retailers in town, was ruining the face of the industry. Israel Diamond Supply and I, personally, were subjected to all possible forms of business harassments. From the Office of the Attorney General to the Better Business Bureau, I was forced to justify many times why I was not charging the consumer more money! Never backing down and always believing I had nothing to fear by doing the right thing, I stood in the face of all obstacles and dismantled them one at a time. At times the task seemed impossible. Not only did I run the business, take care of employees, do inventories, design new rings, and develop new business approaches, but I also had to fight the opposition along the way. It is not easy to be labeled the black sheep because you do not conform to the standard set by retailers. You must charge twice your cost and be like everyone else. What they missed is that I am *not* like everyone else. I have never been a follower, but always a leader, always thinking about how to take a lemon and make lemonade.

Israel Diamond Supply today is the largest-volume diamond store in Oklahoma and one of the largest privately owned stores in the nation. It all started with a mountain man with a vision, who came to the USA with the hope that one day he would have his own orchard. With all the large corporately owned jewelry stores in Oklahoma wondering why they are not doing well, and all the setbacks and disadvantages, I had something that made it all possible: the mind of an entrepreneur and the belief that no matter what anyone said, *I can do it*. My motto? For every action, there is a reaction. Taking action on a bad idea is more productive than not acting on a good idea—the worst possible result is *experience*!

Adel Nasreddine

KEY SUCCESS FACTORS: Action, Action, Action, Passion, Perseverance, Leadership, Customer Service, Price, Volume of Sales

RECOMMENDED BOOKS: *Selling the Invisible* by Harry Beckwith, *Differentiate or Die* by Jack Trout, *Confessions of an Economic*

Hit Man by John Perkins, *Rain Making* by Ford Harding, *How to Win Friends and Influence People* by Dale Carnegie, *The Ten Commandments for Business Failure* by Donald R. Keough, *No B.S. Wealth Attraction for Entrepreneurs* by Dan S. Kennedy

WEB SITE: *www.israeldiamond.com*

EDITOR'S NOTE: Adel Nasreddine lives in Tulsa with his wife and is still working seven days a week at Israel Diamond Supply.

I don't dream at night, I dream all day; I dream for a living.
—Steven Spielberg

CATCHING THE ENTREPRENEURIAL SPIRIT: DREAMS DO COME TRUE

I started my entrepreneurial spirit at a very early age. My sister, Mary Fern Carpenter, in her book entitled *Have I Told You about the Time . . . ?* captures this side of me in the excerpt below.

> When he (Mark) was about seven and I (Mary Fern) was in college, my parents moved to a new neighborhood. After settling in, my parents looked around this quiet area and realized it was quiet because there were no children around. In fact, all of our neighbors in the surrounding blocks were senior citizens. Mark seemed to handle the lack of playmates with aplomb and entertained himself pretty well.
>
> One day when I was home from college, though, I became concerned by his lengthy stay in the bathroom. I alerted Mom. "Mom, do you think maybe Mark is playing mad scientist again?" He liked to make concoctions from the treasures in the medicine cabinet.
>
> Mom tapped on the bathroom door. On the other side of the door, we heard Mark replying sweetly that he would be out in a moment. True to his word, he soon entered the kitchen.
>
> Mother and I stared at him in amazement. There stood this seven-year-old boy dressed to the nines. He had on his black slacks, his white sports coat, and his bow tie. His hair was slicked down and carefully combed. The final touch—he was wearing sunglasses.
>
> We were too shocked to ask. So he announced, "I'm going around to meet my new neighbors."
>
> Speechless, Mom and I watched as Mark walked across the street and knocked on the first door. A white-haired lady answered. Mark extended his hand. Then the lady's husband came out, and he shook hands with Mark too. They took seats on the porch, Mark sitting on the porch swing, and had at least a thirty-minute talk. What they thought about this little boy in a white sports coat, bow tie, and sunglasses, I can only imagine. Mom

and I continued to observe as Mark made his rounds. From that time on, he periodically continued to make those rounds, paying those visits and checking on his neighbors. He loved them all and relished listening to their stories of the past. Without a doubt, they loved him and the courteous attention he paid them.

Now that Mark is grown, his travels have extended beyond a few blocks. But in spite of his wanderings, he is always there for his family and his church family. And even though he is involved in some pretty impressive business ventures, I think he considers his journeys as just going out to meet his neighbors.

As I look back, I believe my parents' hard-work ethic launched my interest in entrepreneurship. My parents were both from blue-collar backgrounds—hardworking, God-fearing, and community servants. My dad, for example, worked as a plumber, electrician, city inspector, hospital maintenance engineer, air-conditioning repairman, plasterer, and owner of a trailer park and a roller-skating rink, to name a few of his jobs. Though he only obtained an eighth grade education, he had the instincts of an entrepreneur and the desire to succeed.

My parents encouraged a strong work ethic. My first job after school and during summers, started at age ten. I picked up trash from around a hospital and surrounding facilities where my dad served as engineer. He believed I needed to learn step-by-step, so the next job he assigned me was janitorial work.

My mother also had various jobs. Her current job is as the museum curator of Old Town Museum in Elk City, Oklahoma, where she has served for over thirty years. Although she recently turned 90 years old, she continues to serve on three boards.

My parents inspired me to learn, to travel, and to aspire to success. Other mentors also encouraged me to reach out and achieve—businessmen, doctors, teachers, preachers, and others. They inspired me to dream. So I dreamed. As a young boy, I dreamed of being active in businesses, movies, and music productions. I wanted to be an author, political activist, songwriter, guitarist, performer, and active in church, along with other pursuits.

Many doors have opened throughout my career. For the most part, by entering open doors, I found great opportunities. Most of my businesses succeeded. My first company was founded when I was twenty-three years old. My partner and I invested $1,000 each. With hard work and determination, the company achieved great success in the oil and gas industry. However, along with successes came failures. Whether it was due to management, economics, or lack of perseverance, some projects just did not survive.

I have learned it is important to never give up, never forget where you came from, and remember all those who inspired you and all those who believed in you. It is important to remember you will not be an expert in everything, so you need knowledgeable advisors. And also of great importance is to become a mentor to others, to share your knowledge, your experiences, and your encouragement.

Now forty years later, I have achieved many of my dreams. I have established several businesses, served on private and public corporate boards and served on university boards. I have attended United States presidential inaugurations after having worked on campaigns. I had the opportunity to meet four United States presidents including President George W. Bush, President Reagan, President George H. Bush, and President Ford. I met with various world leaders including Prime Minister Klaus of Czech Republic, Russian Minister of Energy Yuri Shafranik, Russian leader Gorbachev and others. I have led international business delegation visits and worked on staff for a United States senator. I walked down the red carpet of the 2002 Academy Awards as a guest of then film partner and Academy Award winning producer Gray Fredrickson. I have written two books, produced movies, written songs, and enjoyed performing.

Nancy, my wife, has been supportive of my efforts. We have been married for over thirty-one years, and she has been by my side all the way. Through good, bad, and lean years, I could always count on Nancy. And I have been truly blessed by God to have such a wonderful family, parents, sister, children, and grandchildren.

I am now fifty-three and believe I have forty good work years ahead. Yes, forty to work! This will leave me another seven years for retirement. This is how much I love entrepreneurship. Why quit when so many opportunities lie ahead? By the way, I forgot to mention an important point in describing an entrepreneur. It doesn't hurt to be a little eccentric. Now go out and meet your neighbors!

Mark A. Stansberry

KEY SUCCESS FACTORS: Work Ethic, Dreaming of the Future, Vision, Service, Never Giving Up

RECOMMENDED BOOKS: *The Snowball: Warren Buffet and the Business of Life* by Alice Schroeder, *Hammer* by Armand Hammer, *Never Eat Alone* by Keith Ferrazzi, *Boone* by Boone Pickens

WEB SITES: *www.thegtdgroup.com*, *www.thebrakingpoint.com*, *www.markstansberry.com*

EDITOR'S NOTES: Mark A. Stansberry coauthored the energy handbook *The Acquisition Process and Due Diligence: Minimize Risk/Maximize Return!* In 2008 he authored the book *The Braking Point: America's Energy Dreams and Global Economic Realities*. Mark has led fund-raising efforts for nonprofit and political campaigns. Presently, he serves as cochairman, along with General Tommy Franks, for the Heart of America/Enterprise Square Campaign to raise $10 million. He has been a delegate to three national party conventions. Mark and his wife, Nancy, of Edmond, Oklahoma, are active in their church. They have been married for over thirty years and have three grown children and one granddaughter.

The following story is by Mark's wife, Nancy, from the perspective of an entrepreneur's wife.

LIVING WITH AN ENTREPRENEUR

When I married Mark A. Stansberry over thirty years ago, I knew it would be somewhat different from a "normal" life. I often say we are addicted to adrenaline flow. To be married to an entrepreneur, one needs to be extremely flexible in many areas. The positive side is Mark was able to be at many of our children's programs at school during the day and at other activities a person working on a nine-to-five job might not be able to attend. Entrepreneurs have the flexibility to arrange their schedule to fit their lives, but many times, they are working when others aren't.

As a consultant or as a contract worker, it is possible you will not be paid regularly. At times in the early days, it could be ninety days or longer before he would receive payment for his services. These were the most difficult and stressful times for me as our children were growing up. I became the most frugal of shoppers and learned the value of a dollar and how to get the most out of one! As the successes have grown, payment is no longer a worry; but as the spouse of an entrepreneur starting out, you have to be ready for frugality and know your spouse will probably not be sitting with you in front of the television every evening.

I have directed a competitive children's chorus for the past eight years, and Mark is my assistant. He teaches the children how to get on and off the risers and how to march. We have made *gold* scores each year, and Mark is a major reason why. I love he never lets the fact he has achieved many important things and is a VIP in many arenas keep him from wanting to help others. He loves being a humble servant as often as he can.

Being married to an entrepreneur has many pros and cons, but as time goes on and successes grow, the good far outweighs the bad. It is an exciting life that I feel I was destined for, and I thank God for Mark and our life!

Nancy Stansberry

KEY SUCCESS FACTORS: Dedication, Determination

Pursue your dreams and outrun your fears.
　　　　　　　　　　　—Ruth Lance Wester

ROPIN' THE DREAM

Who would have dreamed a girl who had no brothers would spend her life in a man's world, producing rodeos with her cowboy-roper husband, and live to write the story? After high school, I joined the U.S. Air Force to see the world. As a flight attendant, I saw enough of the Mediterranean Sea from points in North Africa and Italy that coming home to Oklahoma looked mighty good to me.

In November 1961, after a brief courtship, Oklahoma calf roper Ken Lance and I were married in Chicago, where I rode into the arena at the National Cowboy Finals as the Rodeo Princess and rode out as Ken's bride and soon-to-be business partner.

Rodeo was in Ken's blood. "Ruthie," he said, "we could turn this watermelon patch into a rodeo arena in our own backyard." In the summer of 1964, with seed money from my dad, L. L. Whitlock, and the support of Ken's roping partner's dad, Dean Lance, we realized our dream. Hollywood Western star Tim Holt was featured every night in our five-thousand-seat all-steel arena hosting the annual Ada rodeo. Cowboy champions competed with local bull riders and calf ropers. Loretta Lynn sang at the dance in the open-air pavilion nearby.

Ken was roping his dream, and I was riding mine. I quickly learned barrel riding and calf roping were not my winning talents. However, partnering with Ken to produce and promote an affordable family-oriented annual rodeo uncovered other strengths I didn't know I had. While women were burning their bras in the 1960s for equal pay with men, I was burning up the telephone wires, coordinating details with workers, celebrities, and advertising teams—men and women alike.

Being a woman was not an issue. In fact, we awarded cowgirls the same prize money as cowboys at the annual rodeo. All-girl rodeos were held in the fall and spring. The winner took away a Miley horse trailer and the popular Ken Lance shoulder-strap leather purse, which Ken and I made in our saddle shop. Ken sold our last one right off my shoulder.

We roofed the dance pavilion. Throughout the year, we booked local bands for weekly Saturday night dances, and rising stars such as Dottie West for holiday celebrations. Our goal was a bigger and better rodeo every year, featuring such stars as Willie

Nelson, Red Steagall, Reba McEntire, and Barbara Mandrell. Sixteen-time world-champion cowboy Jim Shoulders provided livestock. African American cowboy champion Charles Sampson, three-time world-champion barrel racer Martha Josey, and other champions rode out of the chutes.

Sooner or later, bad luck would fall. Sure enough, one year, we had to cancel the rodeo due to the Equine Encephalitis epidemic in Texas. Livestock were quarantined. Country-and-western musicians performed anyway, but to a much smaller crowd.

Another time, Ken roped a coyote he saw heading for a neighbor's chickens. The coyote bit him when he hog-tied it. The veterinarian packaged the animal's head to send to Oklahoma City to be tested for rabies. However, the package inadvertently was left behind. Rabies vaccine was rushed to Ken, and he had to take the series of shots. But the show must go on. Despite the pain, Ken rode into the arena carrying the American flag, as he always did in opening ceremonies.

The worst was yet to come. A decade later, on Christmas Eve 1981, a drunk driver crashed into the car my sister, June Proctor, was driving in Maryland and killed two of her sons and all three grandbabies. I flew to Maryland for the funeral. The rodeo was never the same for us without our nephews in the grandstand.

Our marriage was already suffering from the year-round stress of producing a rodeo, as the originally dirt-poor cowboy champions climbed to million-dollar prize money and the country-and-western stars hit the multimillionaire top. We could no longer afford to hire them.

In 1986, Ken and I divorced. I moved to Durant, home of Southeastern Oklahoma State University, where I worked as the sales representative for Quality Inn and met my future husband, Dr. John T. Krattiger, retired math professor. In 1993, Ken produced his last rodeo. In 1994, my niece and I attended the Ken Lance Tribute in Ada and bid a tearful farewell to decades of memories.

Later my sister, June, said, "Ruth, this is a part of Oklahoma's cowboy culture history. Someone needs to write a book about it. Why not us? You lived it, and we can write it. Get Ken on the phone." With Ken's help roping in interviews, and with the cowboys and cowgirls, country-and-western singers, and local people who helped to make it all happen, the book came together.

In the meantime, Dr. Krattiger died, and I married his lifelong friend, Dr. Truman Wester, president emeritus of Grayson County College, Denison, Texas. The Ken Lance Sports Arena had been a family project from the beginning, and so it continued with Truman, who coined the phrase "husbands-in-law" to describe his relationship with Ken. Even Ken's wife, Malinda LaVey Clifton, helped me collect the printed materials we needed for research.

In January 2006, the Rodeo Historical Society in Oklahoma City published a bird's-eye view of the book in the *Ketchpen*, Winter Issue. On the twenty-first of September that same year, Ken died unexpectedly at his home. The book, dedicated to the memory of Ken and our fathers, was published in 2007 and was awarded first place by the Press Women of Texas.

People are amazed that while my marriage to Ken did not endure, our friendship outlived death. Truman and I are on the board of directors as founding members of the 3-Crosses/Ken Lance Arena, where youth rodeos and Bible camps are held each summer. We endowed the Ken Lance and Ruth Lance Wester scholarship fund at SOSU, where Truman taught math for several years.

The key to my success was family. Our families believed in our dream and were there for us in good times and bad. The men I married after our divorce were educators who agreed this part of Oklahoma's cowboy history was significant enough to be recorded for posterity. To young entrepreneurs today, I would say, "Pursue your dreams and outrun your fears." It never occurred to me that I couldn't do something new. I just did it.

Ruth Lance Wester and June Proctor

KEY SUCCESS FACTORS: Passion, Determination, Perseverance

RECOMMENDED BOOKS: *The Story of the Ken Lance Sports Arena, 1964-1994* by Ruth Lance Wester and June Proctor

WEB SITE: *www.ruthlancewester.com*

EDITOR'S NOTES: Ruth Lance Wester lives in Denison, Texas, with her husband. She attributes her inspiration and motivation to her father, L. L. Whitlock; her sister, June Proctor; and Ken Lance.

CHAPTER THREE

FINDING A NICHE

When you know what you want and you want it badly enough, you'll find a way to get it.
—Jim Rohn

Do what you can with what you have, where you are.
—Theodore Roosevelt

THE RUGGED ENTREPRENEUR

Having grown up in the small town of Pottsboro, Texas, where cattle population easily exceeds the human population of less than two thousand and the median per capita income was $16,357, I am fortunate enough to have emerged as one of the most successful entrepreneurs in Grayson County. My parents were divorced by the time I was six months old, leaving my mother to raise four kids on her own in a community where many kids didn't make it to college, or even all the way through high school.

Today I own Reedy Fiberglass & Marine, where I do fiberglass repair and painting on boats of all sizes. During twenty-seven years of hard work, I have managed to gain respect for my skills and to offer extraordinary customer service.

One of my first jobs was at an auto shop, where my sole responsibility was to replace car bumpers. The auto shop also offered fiberglass repair, so I quickly became interested in this line of work and watched closely in order to learn this skill. After many years of practicing and performing side jobs on cars, I was approached by Loe's Highport Marina on Lake Texoma to perform numerous fiberglass and gelcoat repair jobs on boats. Not having a desire to work for anyone else but myself, I gave the auto shop a one-month notice.

After a month, I started operating out of my garage at home, which evolved into a large shop and then later into Reedy Fiberglass & Marine on Highport Road. This is the main road that leads to the largest inland marina in the state of Texas.

A difference maker in my success was acting on the importance of "location, location, location," and moving my shop to the prime location where it is now. Located on what might as well be a major interstate highway, a road where thousands of boats and boat owners pass by on a daily basis, my shop attracts numerous customers throughout the year.

Many people have heard the expression "Behind every strong man is an even stronger woman." In no other circumstance is this phrase more relevant than in my relationship with Shelly Reedy. We are the two strongest willed people ever known to mankind. If there was ever anyone who could handle me, it was Shelly.

My contributions are giving back on a small-town scale, but with large-scale benefits. One of my biggest inspirations has been my daughter, Rikki, who is an avid softballer, whose love and enthusiasm for the sport is equally matched by my love for racing. I am also a certified auto trader, which has allowed me to support my daughter's softball teams by providing driving services through my connection with the trading world. Many times, Rikki's softball teams have shown up for competitions in a luxury RV driven by me. Also, in small towns such as Pottsboro, high school football is king; and one of the most important times of the season is homecoming week. During this time, I offer some of my exotic cars for the homecoming queen nominees for the parade. These gifts to the public may not be worth a lot of money, but they hold great value to the recipients.

The definition of an entrepreneur as stated in an online dictionary is "a person who organizes and manages any enterprise, especially a business, usually with considerable initiative and risk." Do I manage a business and take on considerable risks? Yes, of course. I have done this through many years of self-taught motivation. I had no safety net, only the promise to myself to succeed and make a better life for the next generation. Often, I had to rely solely on myself, through both good and bad times, to achieve success by doing things my way. I am proof if you want something badly enough and are willing to put every ounce of your heart and soul into it, then all it takes is for you to go and get *it*. My hope is to be an inspiration for all small-town kids and to influence others to live this dream.

Billy Reedy
Contributed by Justin Hayward

KEY SUCCESS FACTORS: Finding a Niche, Customer Service, Location of Business, Passion

EDITOR'S NOTES: Billy Reedy lives in Texas with his wife, Shelly, and daughter, Rikki.

Coming together is a beginning, staying together is progress, and working together is success.
—Henry Ford

CLEANING UP!

It's always hard to remember how it started. It is also hard to define an entrepreneur. I've embraced the idea an entrepreneur need not necessarily start a business, but rather, may accept and promote change through innovation and empowerment. In my mind, challenging common notions is what entrepreneurship is all about.

It wasn't until after winning the Global Student Entrepreneur Award in 2008 that I knew so many young people wanted to be entrepreneurs. They may not know what business they want to start, but they want to be an entrepreneur. Why would anybody want to voluntarily undergo the pain this weird breed of people go through? Why? Because the rewards are so incredibly overwhelming it is like the ultimate high.

I never called myself an entrepreneur until the majority of my professors, associates, peers, and advisors beat it into my head that I was, in fact, an entrepreneur.

I didn't start a company. I joined one. The company I joined was basically a one-man show. My dedicated business partner, Adam Jacknow, had started a company called Husky Express. The company was a single route for laundry and dry cleaning. Adam called it Husky Express because the Northeastern mascot was a husky. He started the company because he paid to have his laundry done; then his friends asked if they could pay him to have theirs done as well . . . from then on, it was all Tide and Downy for him.

I became involved when I saw an ad for a driver, called up because I needed money for school, and went to an interview. When I met Adam, I was super-intrigued with what this guy was doing. He looked as if he hadn't slept in four days. He was operating this dingy Laundromat and didn't have any idea how much money he made, but he loved it. I had come from New York, where I worked in a lavish Wall Street law firm and delivered pizza on the side instead of going to class. Husky Express seemed like a change in scenery, but I never saw myself there for more than one year. I immediately got into an eight-hour conversation with Adam about how to improve marketing, operations, finance, etc.

I had always helped my mom run her small business in New York, and I had run a couple of my own. I was always a hustler in spirit, so this new company seemed fun. After one month, I moved from delivery to the back office and convinced Adam to hire another driver so I could build the business with him. I created project after project to shore up systems and work on the areas that were not Adams strengths. Funny thing is, Adam and I—to this date—have complemented each other's skill sets but continue to reverse roles from time to time.

The company revenues were approximately $100,000 per year back then. Today, five years later, revenues are approaching $1 million. It is an amazing accomplishment to look back with respect to revenue, milestones, and employment. In five years, we have hired a great staff, invented a digital locker system for secure delivery of garments, created a robust online tracking portal for deliveries and special requests, and made the news multiple times. Sounds like pure glory, right? Well, to a certain extent it was. What was I if I was not an entrepreneur?

I was a salesman, an operator, an accountant, a driver at times, a software QA/story liner, a negotiator, a legal advisor . . . overall, I was a problem solver. It wasn't until people started calling me entrepreneur that I realized what I had become. There was a lot of stress because I was always the behind-the-scenes guy; and all of a sudden, I was out beating the pavement as the CEO, trying to raise the half million we needed to fuel growth to profitability.

A very respected and wise guy once told me, "It is all about living on the edge and the lessons you learn when you are there." If you are never in your comfort zone, you are on the edge. The edge is great, but it is also dangerous. As long as you are living in sync with your values and you can handle the peaks and valleys, then this is right for you. Never once start to think being an entrepreneur is easy or that it's about not having a boss. When you run your own company, you have many bosses: investors, customers, and even your employees' needs. I wouldn't choose anything else in the world. But be prepared to ignore the end goal, enjoy the fight, and embrace the stress the whole way . . . otherwise, you'll run out of energy to channel into your baby (company).

Dominic Coryell

KEY SUCCESS FACTORS: Finding a Niche, Staying Out of My Comfort Zone

RECOMMENDED BOOK(S): *LifeManual* by Peter Thomas, *Winning* by Jack Welch, *Road Rules* by Andrew Sherman, *Little Red Book of Sales* by Jeffrey Gittomer, *First 100 Days of Selling* by Jim Ryerson

WEB SITE: *www.garmentvalet.com*

EDITOR'S NOTES: Dominic Coryell is currently a senior at Northeastern University in Boston, Massachusetts. He will continue his operations at Garment Valet following graduation, with plans to embark on a national expansion in 2010. Revenues in 2008 exceeded $900,000 with just over 1,900 customers. Garment Valet has a goal of quadrupling its customer base in 2009, now that the platform for the software can handle customers seamlessly. Dominic was awarded the 2008 Global Student Entrepreneur title by Entrepreneurs' Organization (EO).

He who reigns within himself and rules his passions, desires, and fears is more than a king.
—*John Milton*

BUILDING A BIG, MINIATURE EMPIRE

Success and entrepreneurship don't just fall into your lap—*you make* them happen. The beauty of life is that almost nothing can hold you back. *The Tonight Show* host Jay Leno once stated, "Perseverance wins over genius 99 percent of the time." You've got to take the bull by the horns and simply *do* it. This is how it all started for me:

Born and raised in Southern California, I was always a railroad enthusiast. From an early age, my close proximity to railroad tracks inspired me to learn more about the railroads—what they do, what they haul, and every other aspect of the business. I didn't know it then, but this understanding would be my first business strength.

One thing I can't stress enough for any entrepreneur is *passion*. When you put in long hours for weeks, months, and even years, you *need* passion to keep you motivated. When you do something you love, it doesn't seem like work; and you'll find a great sense of pride knowing you're producing or delivering a service you actually enjoy. I consider passion as a business strength.

During 2000, at age fifteen, I started custom-painting locomotives for people all over the world. I posted on Internet forums, gained word-of-mouth recognition, and built up a client list of over one hundred customers. After learning the aspects of the industry by working for several different companies, I applied my keen sense of both the industry and the market to quickly establish BLMA Models as a fresh, innovative company. At that point, I began producing (through outside contract manufacturers) small locomotive and scenery accessories.

Because I didn't have any investment capital (I was barely sixteen years old), I used the profits from my current products to fund future projects. I was always working one or two part-time jobs, which helped develop my business knowledge. I highly recommend having as many jobs as possible to learn from others strengths and weaknesses.

As time passed and the product line expanded, I stopped custom painting to focus strictly on mass-produced scenery and locomotive accessories. At this point, I contacted my first distributor. After much patience and communication, the distributor picked up my entire product line. From there, the process of getting the product into stores and advertising really came into play. If you're selling a product, I recommend getting in with a major distributor as soon as possible!

BLMA Models now boasts a line of two hundred-plus products in multiple scales, five distributors, and access through thousands of hobby dealers worldwide. All products are researched and designed by BLMA Models employees; however, production is split between two factories in China. I have visited the Chinese factories to ensure quality, pricing, and delivery objectives are met. BLMA Models currently has two full-time employees with multiple part-time employees.

Now that I am twenty-three, the business has developed concurrently with my education at Cal State University, Fullerton, California. I'm majoring in Advertising, with a minor in Business Administration, which I feel will help with building the business for years to come. The success of BLMA Models can be attributed to my formal education, combined with the applied knowledge I've obtained from running the company.

Currently, BLMA Models has expanded to producing rolling stock for the model train market—something I consider the logical next step in growing the business. With the continued success of BLMA Models, I plan to expand into different markets using current and future manufacturing techniques and years of applied experience.

Life is all about learning. In fact, I would say a life without learning is a life without value. In life and business, we must learn from our mistakes and the mistakes of others—why reinvent the wheel if you don't have to? My point is everything should be a growing experience; embrace every opportunity to expand your boundaries.

While I have learned a great deal from my business, a few key points have facilitated my success:

1. **Communication**

    Communication is probably the single most relevant weakness everyone battles in life. We're all different, and we all communicate differently. Great communicators are able to spread their vision, motivate others, and accomplish goals. I regularly step back and think about a simple question: What is my point, and how efficiently can I get this message to my audience? Whether it's with marketers, sales professionals, or simply family, make sure you're doing a good job of explaining your point as it pertains to the audience.

2. **Quality**
Quality should permeate every aspect of your business. On the deepest level, every little aspect of your business contributes to its overall success: your product or service, your packaging, your Web site, the photos on your Web site, how conveniently your Web site is laid out, how you present yourself in person—the list goes on. My point is to set your standards as high as possible—this really is up to you!

3. **Persistence**
Never give up. Those who keep focused on their strengths are the ones who accomplish their goals over time. Even through tough times, you must continually keep your focus to build on your strengths.

4. **Attitude**
Surround yourself with people with great attitudes. Aspire to the highest levels you can, and don't let small things get in your way. If you're motivated and happy, the success will come so long as you put your efforts in productive ideas.

5. **Values**
You must develop a core set of values on which you base your life and business decisions. While we hear the saying "Business is business," and that is true to some extent, there are actual *people* working in every business. Make sure you treat people the way *they* want to be treated, and make sure you hold your values over time.

6. **Mentors**
Sometimes I don't feel like going to events or reaching outside my comfort zone; however, for myself and those of you like me, we must *get over it*. Every time I have pushed

myself to attend or be a part of an event, I have always walked away a better, more experienced person. I can't stress enough that the mentors and connections you make will help your business and personal life exponentially—that is, *if* you use them effectively. Don't be a stranger; feel free to call people, shoot e-mails, or set up lunch dates. You really have nothing to lose, and people love it when you take an interest in them.

I'll close by saying you have the power to do anything you want. Business is about pushing the boundaries, working on your strengths, broadening your horizons, and making your own success a reality. You have the ability, so find something you love, and go after it. It's been said many times before: entrepreneurship really is the best job in the world. I wish you all the best.

Craig Martyn

KEY SUCCESS FACTORS: Communication, Quality, Persistence, Attitude, Values, Mentors

RECOMMENDED BOOKS: *Buzzmarketing* by Mark Hughes, *Sales Octane* by Jim Ryerson

WEB SITE: *www.blmamodels.com*

EDITORS NOTE: While the success of BLMA Models has catapulted Craig into the business world, he is concurrently pursuing his next venture—a marketing company devoted to producing miniature versions of major products. With continued success, Craig hopes to also get into the commercial real estate business in the near future.

What we think or what we know or what we believe is, in the end, of little consequence. The only consequence is what we do.
—*John Ruskin*

H IS FOR HONESTY

I've always been an odd combination of humanitarian and entrepreneur, but I never thought I'd be running around from podium to podium, giving lectures on humanitarian design and social entrepreneurship. Yet here I am, twenty-seven years old and the founder of Project H Design, a nonprofit that's (hopefully) changing the way the world thinks about product design.

At six years old, I began developing little businesses—garage sales, lemonade stands, and even a weekly coin hunt, where my sister and I would clean the house by searching the couches for loose change. My father saw entrepreneurship in my nature and instigated assignments to help me develop my business side. When I wanted to get a pet rat, my father requested a business proposal outlining the reasons I'd be a good rat owner. When I traveled to Mexico and Belize to volunteer in high school, I presented a fund-raising request to family and friends on letterhead with bulleted lists showing what the donations would do and what they'd get out of donating (usually cookies). By the end of high school, I knew three things: I was a creative thinker, a humanitarian, and an entrepreneur. I pursued a career in Architecture, and ultimately Industrial Design—and that's where my story really starts.

Industrial Design is the art of making products that work within an everyday lifestyle. Hopefully, they go beyond just consumption to solve problems and enable life in efficient and beautiful ways. It was the perfect outlet for my creativity, my inventiveness, and my entrepreneurial nature. I poured myself into learning Industrial Design, hoping to make things that mattered, told stories, and made life better.

As part of my graduate thesis, I designed a Human Nest Chair—a handmade bowl-shaped chair exploding with thousands of soft, colorful recycled fabric scraps designed to engage and comfort the owner. It was a social commentary and critique on our usual slick and shiny consumer culture. I instead wanted to design heirlooms, things that were personal and nostalgic. I didn't expect the chair to become a retail product, as it was just a part of my uberconceptual thesis. But at my graduate exhibit, I was met with "How much are they?" and "Great, I'll take one." Without planning on it, I'd started a furniture business called Emily Pilloton Designs.

I started making chairs by the order, spending fifty to sixty hours perfecting each Human Nest; but I felt incredibly unsatisfied. And as with many businesses, there was one single moment that changed everything. While in my attic studio working on an order for Neiman Marcus, I had an epiphany: This was not the kind of design I had set out to do, and it was certainly not true to the original intention of my thesis. I didn't want to make $2,000 chairs for rich people because, I believed, industrial design should be more about problem solving than simply creating a craft. Something had been lost along the way.

Call it rebellion, or call it philosophy, but I've never cowered to a mainstream directive and have always held true to my own instincts. So I closed Emily Pilloton Designs.

I began unlearning things I had been taught in graduate school and began designing the way I wanted to design. I also started writing for various blogs and design magazines known for criticizing the profitable side of industrial design. "Do we really need to produce more luxury items?" I'd ask my readers. "What's the real definition of industrial design?" I became the managing editor of Inhabitat—an online green design publication. During my time with Inhabitat, the blog's readership grew exponentially based on my critical focus. Within months, I developed a huge network of support and found thousands of designers agreed with me. And most importantly, I figured out what I really wanted to do was create products designed for a different client: the disempowered and overlooked—those traditionally ignored by design. I saw the developing world, children, the disabled, the elderly, the homeless, and others, as the true design client. These were the demographics that could benefit most from ingenious design solutions.

At that time, I had $400 and was living at my parents' house; but I started a company called Project H Design focused on design for the *Hs*—humanity, habitats, health, and happiness. I created a simple blog-style Web site featuring examples of industrial designs meeting the needs of a greater good. What began as a blog quickly turned into a more action-based entity.

In early 2008, I made a call to my community of readers: "We need the design world to stop talking big and start doing good with design for health, poverty, homelessness, and education. We need to turn our tightly clinched consumer business models and luxury aesthetics on their heads and focus on appropriate solutions for basic problems (power, water, health care). We need to reconsider who our clients really are and to enlist a new generation of design activists."

Hundreds of designers wrote to me, saying, "We agree, we're convinced, we want to do this, and we'll do it for free. But how does it work?" Without a business plan and relying simply on my instinct, I registered Project H as a nonprofit and got to work.

We set up city chapters where young designers who were passionate about the idea of changing something (rather than making money) could engage with their communities using their design skills. Partnerships with local organizations resulted in therapeutic solutions for a foster care home in Austin, a homeless-run design cooperative in Los Angeles, and more. In March of 2008, Project H launched its first large fund-raising and design initiative—the Hippo Roller.

The Hippo Roller, originally designed by two South African men, has improved water transportation for poor communities in South Africa. It employs a simple rolling barrel that holds twenty-four gallons of water—nearly eight times more than traditional methods of transporting water. In two months, we raised $7,500 to fund the delivery of seventy-five Hippo Rollers to the Kgautswane community. Since then, in partnership with Engineers Without Borders, we've redesigned the Hippo Roller to increase shipping efficiency, lower the price point, and fix a few structural flaws.

Our biggest funding breakthrough came in October 2008 when Project H was awarded $10,000 from an entrepreneurial Web site called ideablob.com. Ideablob sponsors a monthly contest where the business idea with the most votes wins start-up funding. Project H unified—sending out e-mails and blog calls and using our network to get votes—*and we did it*. We assembled a design team, including our first-ever intern, a talented design student from Holland, and members of the New York chapter. We developed the Learning Landscape—a grid-based math playground with ten interactive games that would facilitate elementary math education for the Kutamba AIDS Orphans School in Uganda. We installed the playground in January 2009, using tires and play equipment. The playground was a huge success, and we're currently developing a desktop-sized version of the Learning Landscape for in-classroom, tabletop use.

Project H is just over one year old, and our plans are to build a worldwide coalition of like-minded designers and to get out there and do it. Over the past year, we've been published in about fifty magazines and blogs. We've grown to four hundred members in eight chapters, and I've spoken at dozens of events and conferences worldwide. When asked about my secret, my answer is really very simple: I'm doing what I want to do. I'm not following anyone's rules; and in finding my passion, I found my business.

Emily Pilloton
Contributed by Elisabeth Garson

KEY SUCCESS FACTORS: Optimism, Authenticity, Passion, Stubbornness, Not Settling, Pigtails

RECOMMENDED BOOKS: *The Giving Tree* by Shel Silverstein, *The Joy of Cooking* by Irma Rombauer, *Les Misérables* by Victor Hugo, *Design for the Real World* by Victor Papanek

WEB SITE: *www.projecthdesign.com*

EDITOR'S NOTES: At age twenty-seven, Emily Pilloton has found her calling, but will never quell her entrepreneurial spirit. In addition to being the founder and executive director of Project H Design, Emily is also a freelance writer, a furniture designer, and the owner of dozens of Web site domain names for side-project business ideas. She's trained in architecture and industrial design with degrees from UC Berkeley and the School of the Art Institute of Chicago, and has taught design theory in Chicago. When she isn't working, Emily enjoys baking cupcakes and playing trivia board games.

Whether you think you can or whether you think you can't, you're right.

—Henry Ford

A STRONG HEART AND A "NEVER QUIT" ATTITUDE

Deciding to be an entrepreneur is a process, not something with which I awakened. Emotions rise and fall during the process of deciding to become an entrepreneur and continue to rise and fall throughout the entrepreneurial experience. Achieving success requires a strong heart and a "never quit" attitude.

I started working toward owning my own company in the 1990s, shortly after graduating from college. Although many of my jobs were in management, I somehow wasn't satisfied; I wanted more. But before going farther, I need to take you back to the 1980s and give you some history.

I was blessed with the opportunity to serve in the U.S. Navy and learn a lot about myself. I worked on computers and aviation electronics, carrying on my desire to work on and program computers. Not only did I get to work on computers and aircraft, but I was also able to travel around the world and expand my views of the world in which we live. My favorite countries to visit were England, Scotland, Italy, Greece, and Israel.

I left the Navy in 1987 and became an assistant manager for a rent-to-own company. In 1991, I started college with the purpose of serving in the U.S. Marshals. Unfortunately, that dream couldn't become a reality because of my age. However, I graduated Cum Laude in Criminology with an Associates of Science Degree in Criminal Justice.

I married my soul mate in May of 1994 and completed college in December of 1994. Two years later, after joining the U.S. Navy Reserves, I had the opportunity to develop Web sites for the Navy. Although I enjoyed developing Web sites, I wasn't sure whether I wanted to open my own business full-time. Rather than opening my business full-time, I developed Web sites on the side while maintaining a full-time job to help pay the bills and keep food on the table.

It took me four years to break out of my comfort zone and develop Web sites full-time. When I broke out of my comfort zone, I followed a path that would make me an expert in the field by working with a couple of work groups with the World Wide Web Consortium (W3C), helping to come up with the standards used to develop Web sites. This work led to a congressional appointment to the Oklahoma Electronic Commerce Task Force and a gubernatorial appointment to the Oklahoma Electronic and Information Technology Accessibility Task Force. Both appointments allowed me to participate in developing laws and guidelines governing Oklahoma's Web sites and portals.

In 2003, I brought in a partner and developed the Apple Pie Shopping Cart. After a couple of years, my partner decided to take the newest software and the programmers and leave me empty-handed. My immediate thoughts swarmed around the idea that they, overnight, had destroyed the business I spent nine years building. I felt devastated! The situation demanded I make a decision. My two options were to give up and close the business or maintain what I had and build upon it. Even though the world was crumbling around me, I didn't give up; I persevered and began to advance my company.

Realizing the business rested upon relationships I had built and controlled, I started looking for solutions to my problem—a lack of programmers. I still had my customers. It took me a couple of weeks to find replacements and continue development of my software, but my software eventually gained international recognition as the most search-engine-friendly shopping cart in the world, and people from many countries wanted to use it.

A year later, my world came crumbling down again. Attorneys representing a company in California sent me a letter demanding that I cease using the name *Apple*. I asked myself, *How can a small company like mine that develops e-commerce software and Web sites be a target of this large corporation?* My attorneys wanted $500,000 to defend my right to use the word *Apple* in *Apple Pie Shopping Cart*. This time I faced the decision of giving up or finding some way to continue the business.

I consulted my closest confidant, my wife. With her support and the help of a trusted advisor, we came up with a new name—Merchant Metrix. I knew it would take some time to rebrand the company and get people to trust the new name, but I began immediately.

Over the next four years, the business took on a life of its own. Merchant Metrix continues to evolve and advance in the marketplace. We've increased the number of clients using our software and have hired additional employees. In the past two years, we've filed two patent applications for e-commerce processes. The first ensures we maintain the U.S. title of the most search-engine-friendly shopping cart available. The second brings a new method of marketing to e-commerce businesses, one we feel will help online stores increase their revenue while continuing to decrease their advertising costs.

I can't close my story without explaining that I could not have gotten through or done any of this without the assistance of my Father in Heaven. I can testify that following his commandments and paying one's tithe will bring rewards far too many to count. I am blessed to have Judy in my life, and our love for each other helps us grow closer together.

Surviving the entrepreneur experience requires heart and a "never quit" attitude. One simply cannot succeed without both of these qualities. A strong heart and emotional stability will help you get through tough times, and the "never quit" attitude will ensure you get through the adversity. Learn from the lessons placed in your path, and ask God for assistance when you need it; he's waiting to help.

Lee Roberts

KEY SUCCESS FACTORS: Faith, Strong Heart, "Never Quit" Attitude, Positive Thinking, Judy

RECOMMENDED BOOKS: The Holy Bible, *The Book of Mormon*, *The 21 Irrefutable Laws of Leadership* by John C. Maxwell

WEB SITE: *www.merchantmetrix.com*

EDITOR'S NOTES: Lee Roberts has been a computer technician, network administrator, and programmer since 1978. He has taught Web site design at local technical colleges and written over one hundred articles about Internet marketing and search engine optimization. The first step to success is "believe in yourself and then convince others to believe in you too." Despite the downturn in the economy, the Merchant Metrix team is increasing sales and revenue for the company.

When you cannot make up your mind which of two evenly balanced courses of action you should take—choose the bolder.

—*W. J. Slim*

THE ACCIDENTAL ENTREPRENEUR

If you get excited when you e-mail someone in the middle of the night and they respond immediately, you might be an entrepreneur.

If you get anxious if you haven't worked (or thought about work) for more than an hour, you might be an entrepreneur.

If you spend vacations pitching new business ideas to your wife, you might be an entrepreneur.

If thinking about working for someone else makes you sick to your stomach, you might be an entrepreneur.

One thing was for sure—I was *not* going to work any longer for the guy who employed me. So I started a company.

At twenty-five, I naively thought I could do this on my own. It would take work, sure, but it allowed me to control my own destiny. On a sheet of paper, I wrote down the basic tenets for starting a public relations, public affairs, and strategic marketing firm. I had evaluated my target market and was confident a need existed for the types of services that suited my skill set. Competition was minimal, and I figured I could survive even if I made mistakes. Besides, I've never been one to be concerned about what the other guy was doing.

My entrepreneurial father said, "Go for it." My pragmatic mother opined on the difficulty of attending grad school *and* starting a company. I broke it to her gently that grad school was off. She wasn't thrilled with my reasoning. The truth is, I figured if I screwed up and failed, I'd have a good story the first day of class. My future wife, LeeAnne, said she believed in me, which inspired me enough to get going. Fear of failure wasn't on the table. Six years later, Saxum Public Relations is the largest PR firm in our market and a leader in our region, with revenues of $2 million and a strong foundation for future growth. This is a story in progress.

I had no idea what I was doing—not that I let anyone know it. Admittedly, I liked to make my own decisions and could be hardheaded about the direction I thought we should go. That's a good thing most of the time. But I was young and inexperienced and making recommendations that affected my clients' bottom line. The good news is most of those decisions turned out to be right, and our reputation grew. I wasn't afraid of making mistakes and always learned something when I messed up. I often said I was turning traditional PR upside down. Whatever people usually did, I recommended they do the opposite. It worked.

By the time we were two years old, I employed eight people and had a million dollars in revenue and woke up with the realization that I didn't know how to manage people. It took some time for me to grasp the key to building a good public relations firm: understanding our products are people's ideas. Those ideas are in brains and on laptops—and both go home at night, which is why leadership is so important.

Basically, I believe three things about leadership: (1) people want to be led, (2) people will run through a wall for you if they believe you truly appreciate their contributions, and (3) many people will not have as high expectations for themselves as you have for them. Therefore, an honest approach to encourage people's strengths and improve weaknesses has always been my style.

Financially, we have been profitable since day one. An early mistake I made was taking on an equity partner who provided cash to pay my measly salary and fund client acquisition costs. I gave up 50 percent of the business to someone who had little impact in helping us achieve my goals. The good news is after four years, I was able to purchase his shares at a handsome profit to him. An expensive lesson, for sure, but one I needed. In retrospect, I could have started my business with a $20,000 credit facility.

There are two areas I've focused on to sustain our 20 percent-plus annual growth. Since my expectations for myself and our company are high and I despise losing, I have always been honest with myself about my strengths and weaknesses. In the areas where I struggle—and there are many of them—I've tried to surround myself with people who are stronger than me. Several of those key people have been with me since near the beginning. Secondly, I believe the best leaders and the fastest-growing companies have an innate sense of how to prioritize the importance of tasks. I cannot tell you how many people struggle with these two key areas. One, they are not honest about their individual weaknesses because they are the boss. Two, they focus on accomplishing the wrong things. What was important yesterday is often not the most important task for today.

I consider myself immensely blessed. Our firm is good at figuring out how to help others communicate more effectively with different audiences, and our clients need help communicating. A partnership is formed when we can match our skills with their needs. It's pretty simple. Our best relationships start out strong because both of us understand a partnership is a two-way street requiring passionate participation and spirited discussion to get results. We never pretend to know more than someone about their business. We just apply our strengths, knowledge, and experience to their strategy or given task.

C. Renzi Stone

KEY SUCCESS FACTORS: Valuing People, Prioritizing Tasks, Communication

RECOMMENDED BOOKS: *The Rise of the Creative Class: And How It's Transforming Work, Leisure, Community and Everyday Life* by Richard Florida, *Beyond Basketball: Coach K's Keywords for Success* by Mike Krzyzewski and Jamie K. Spatola, *The Tipping Point: How Little Things Can Make a Big Difference* by Malcolm Gladwell, *Good to Great* by Jim Collins

WEB SITES: *www.saxumpr.com*, *www.saxumpr.blogspot.com*, and *www.twitter.com/renzistone33*

EDITOR'S NOTES: C. Renzi Stone lives with his wife, Lee Anne, in Oklahoma City; they have two sons, Jackson and Isaiah, as well as a dog, Annabelle. In his spare time, he enjoys traveling, reading, hanging out with his family, cheering on the Sooners and Thunder, as well as pitching the occasional new business idea to his wife.

CHAPTER FOUR

TAKING ACTION

Commitment leads to action. Action brings your dream closer.

—*Marcia Wieder*

Success seems to be connected to action. Successful people keep moving. They make mistakes, but they don't quit.

—*Conrad Hilton*

A TRUE ENTREPRENEUR

I was having dinner with my thirty-year-old daughter, Jennifer, on Father's Day in June of 2005. She had invited me for a father-daughter date at a top-notch local steak house in North Atlanta. She knew I was somewhat down in the dumps as a result of my company's current performance.

As the chairman and CEO of Simmons Mattress Company, I had allowed the company to get off track by improperly testing a new product, HealthSmart. This product had a zip-off cover and was designed to attract consumers to our products with a focus on the unsanitary issues that exist in bedding. To some extent, we had bet the ranch on this product idea, and the product was not selling anywhere close to our expectations. As a result, our sales, units, and earnings were all in decline.

After thirty-five years in business, I had achieved financial success and had become well known in the business world as a turnaround manager, focused on cleaning up other people's mess. This time, the mess was mine.

Knowing I had a firefight in front of me, I proceeded to tell Jennifer that I thought it might be time for me to step aside. I began to explain in detail how hard it would be to get the company back on track.

Jennifer listened closely to my sob story and then looked me right in the eye over our martinis and asked, "Would you like my advice?" With hesitation, I said, "Sure." She said, "I think you need to quit feeling sorry for yourself and get back in there and get the job done and finish your career strong." We both shed some tears, and I said, "Thanks, sweetie. That is good advice."

I woke up the next morning and grabbed the bull by the horns. I worked closely with my Executive Vice President of Human Resources to rearchitect the product development, sales, and marketing departments. I began a search for a new EVP of Operations. I made a major change at the executive level, terminating a close friend who had let me down as president of the company with his "my way or the highway" approach.

I began calling all of our major customers to ask for their support and advice while at the same time apologizing for my errors.

I brought in a team of consultants to help me and my new team design a more effective way to sell, promote, and train retail associates on our products.

We rapidly redesigned products, eliminating the HealthSmart feature and going back to our more basic Beautyrest design.

Things started to turn around much quicker than we had expected. There was new energy and commitment that had been absent as I had taken my eye off the ball, delegating too much authority to the wrong people.

As the year passed, all of the numbers turned positive. In December, I chartered two private jets (since not all of us could fly on the same plane) for my senior team, and we held meetings with all of our sales and marketing people, starting in Los Angeles, then flying to Houston, Tampa, and, finally, Atlanta.

I stood in front of every person and said, "I am sorry, and thanks for sticking with us." I also announced a new sales organizational structure that enabled our sales force to spend more time with retailers and also gave each individual an opportunity to earn more money.

In 2006 and 2007, we posted record years. Since the second quarter of 2005, the company has gained market share in fifteen straight quarters.

I have never been a quitter and will be forever grateful to our wonderful daughter for helping me see the light. "It's what you learn after you know it all that counts."

I have been an entrepreneur my whole life, beginning with the first candy stand I set up in front of my house at seven years old.

This is only one of the many stories of failure followed by learning. Remember: never ever give up on yourself.

Charlie Eitel

KEY SUCCESS FACTORS: Determination, Perseverance, Listening, Taking Action

RECOMMENDED BOOKS: *Eitel Time: Turnaround Secrets* by Charlie Eitel; *Mapping Your Legacy: A Hook It Up Journey* by Charlie Eitel; *Value Quotes* by Charlie Eitel

WEB SITE: *www.simmons.com*

EDITOR'S NOTE: Charlie Eitel is currently the Vice Chairman of Simmons Bedding Company and lives in Atlanta, Georgia, and Naples, Florida, with his wife, Cindy.

I think there is something more important than believing: Action! The world is full of dreamers, there aren't enough who will move ahead and begin to take concrete steps to actualize their vision.

—W. Clement Stone

DR. K

I have been surrounded by small businesses and entrepreneurs since I can remember. In my early days growing up in Chicago, my father (Donald W. Kuratko) founded a family business that I was a part of during and after college. Later in my young adulthood, my brother and I developed a limousine business and a consulting firm for smaller businesses. However, after graduating from college, I was surprised at how little I had learned about running a small business. I was provided all the knowledge I needed to work at a corporate office such as General Electric, but was not educated to run a business like the one I grew up with in Chicago.

Frustrated by the lack of concern in traditional business education for smaller ventures, I became committed to developing course work that would teach students who wanted to take the entrepreneurial path what they needed to know. During my MBA studies, I focused completely on the challenges confronting smaller ventures. In pursuing my PhD, I chose the same focus for my research efforts; however, most professors warned me that there was no place in academia for such a focus on small business and entrepreneurial ventures. They were correct! At that time, only a handful of schools offered anything that resembled education for entrepreneurs. Undaunted, I continued to pursue my vision. After completing my PhD, I interviewed at numerous universities, only to be laughed at by most of the schools. One school did not laugh; the people there took the idea seriously. Dr. William R. LaFollette at Ball State University (Muncie, Indiana) believed in my ideas and offered me an opportunity to start an entrepreneurship program. This began my career as an entrepreneurship educator—actually, an *Academic Entrepreneur*.

Like every true entrepreneur, I raised all the money myself to support the entrepreneurship program which I founded at Ball State University. The surging interest in entrepreneurship during the 1980s caused universities to rethink their original stance on the subject, and programs were developed in great numbers. During my years at Ball State University, I created an entrepreneurship program, which eventually became recognized by *U.S. News & World Report* as one of the top four entrepreneurship programs in the nation. In the early '80s, I wrote my first book dealing with small business management. It was 1985 when I conceived the idea for a textbook that would present and develop the pedagogy for the emerging field of entrepreneurship (different from the standard principles in small business management). Once again, I was laughed at, this time by most of the nation's major publishers. Determined to complete my dream, I wrote the entire manuscript (over 550 pages) and offered it to a publisher, stating I would not take any royalties if they would simply publish the book. Harcourt Brace took a chance and published the first edition in 1989. Today *Entrepreneurship: Theory, Process, and Practice* is one of the best-selling entrepreneurship books in the world, as evidenced by being used in over 350 universities and awarded the Australian Award for Excellence in Education Publishing.

Throughout the decade of the '90s, all of the major universities began to take a greater interest in the field of entrepreneurship, and I began to dream again, this time of advancing to the next plateau. I wanted to take my entrepreneurial message to one of the best universities in the world. All of my efforts paid off when I was contacted by Indiana University-Bloomington, a Big Ten institution with a top ten business school. Dr. Dan Smith (Dean of IU's Kelley School of Business) and Dr. Tricia McDougall (Associate Dean of IU's Kelley School of Business), impressed with my career entrepreneurial efforts, recruited me to develop their entrepreneurship program and lead it to become one of the world's best. It was my dream coming true as I accepted the Jack M. Gill Chair of Entrepreneurship and Professor of Entrepreneurship, as well as the position of Executive Director of the Johnson Center for Entrepreneurship and Innovation in the Kelley School of Business at Indiana University-Bloomington. The Indiana University Entrepreneurship Program immediately began to grow by finding the very best research professors in the field of entrepreneurship, and today IU claims the largest entrepreneurship faculty in the world. Under my leadership, Indiana University has achieved the pinnacle of academic recognition: the number one public university ranking for graduate and undergraduate programs in entrepreneurship according to *U.S. News & World Report*. I still continually raise private dollars to supplement the support I receive from IU's Kelley School of

Business so I can expedite the growth and development of the entrepreneurship program.

I absolutely love representing Indiana University around the country as I meet with alumni and supporters to share my entrepreneurial vision and ask for their support. But my dreams don't stop there. I am still interested in expanding entrepreneurial thinking, not only throughout the rest of the Kelley School of Business, but also throughout the entire campus at Indiana University. I have established satellite offices of the Johnson Center for Entrepreneurship and Innovation with IU's Multidisciplinary Sciences, School of Medicine, Maurer School of Law, Jacobs School of Music, School of Informatics, and the IU High Tech Incubator (where I established a student "venture accelerator" to expand students' entrepreneurial ideas). I have created my dream vision at Indiana University: *The Entrepreneurial Campus of the 21st Century!*

Along my entrepreneurial journey, I advised and assisted numerous university entrepreneurial centers such as Miami University, Xavier University, Northern Kentucky University, University of Hawaii, John Carroll University, University of Akron, Baylor University, and Bowling Green State University. In addition, I have been a consultant on Corporate Innovation and Entrepreneurial Strategies to a number of major corporations: WellPoint, AT&T, United Technologies, Walgreens, Union Carbide, SPX, McKesson, ServiceMaster, TruServ, and many others.

I am so proud to say I have helped pioneer the discipline of entrepreneurship into collegiate classrooms across the United States, and now the world. It is so gratifying to look back and now realize all of those who laughed at my dreams were merely blind to the powerful potential that was inherent in entrepreneurship. I truly believe entrepreneurship is the most powerful force we have ever witnessed on this planet. It will always be my passion to mold my students' future and help them follow their entrepreneurial dreams!

Dr. K's Prescriptions:

The entrepreneurial dream is always up to each individual. Here are two of my favorite quotes that depict that belief:

> People are always blaming their circumstances for what they are. I don't believe in circumstances. The people who get on in this world are the people who get up and look for the circumstances they want, and, if they don't find them, make them. (George Bernard Shaw)
>
> To move the world, we must first move ourselves. (Socrates)

I believe the future belongs to those individual entrepreneurs who pursue their visions today.

Donald F. Kuratko

KEY SUCCESS FACTORS: Taking Action, Passion, Pursuing Your Vision

RECOMMENDED BOOKS: *Entrepreneurship: Theory, Process, and Practice* by Donald F. Kuratko, *Corporate Entrepreneurship and Innovation* by Michael H. Morris, Donald F. Kuratko, and Jeffrey G. Covin, *New Venture Management* by Donald F. Kuratko and Jeffrey S. Hornsby.

WEB SITE: *www.kelley.indiana.edu/jcei*

EDITOR'S NOTES: Dr. Donald F. Kuratko (known as Dr. K) is the Jack M. Gill Chair of Entrepreneurship and Professor of Entrepreneurship and the Executive Director of the Johnson Center for Entrepreneurship and Innovation at the Kelley School of Business, Indiana University-Bloomington. Professor Kuratko is considered a prominent scholar and national leader in the field of entrepreneurship. He has published over 160 articles on aspects of entrepreneurship and corporate innovation and he has authored twenty-four books, including some of the leading entrepreneurship books used in universities across the globe today such as *Entrepreneurship: Theory, Process, and Practice,* eighth ed. (Cengage/South-Western Publishers), *Corporate Entrepreneurship and Innovation*, second ed. (SouthWestern/Thomson Publishers), and *New Venture Management* (Pearson/Prentice Hall Publishers).

Dr. Kuratko also cofounded and is currently the Executive Director of the Global Consortium of Entrepreneurship Centers (GCEC), an organization comprising over 250 top university entrepreneurship centers throughout the world. Among his many honors, Dr. Kuratko was named by his peers in *Entrepreneur* magazine as the Number One Entrepreneurship Program Director in the nation, and the National Academy of Management honored Professor Kuratko with the highest award bestowed in entrepreneurship—the prestigious Entrepreneurship Advocate Award—for his contributions to the development and advancement of the discipline of entrepreneurship. His work truly has had a global impact!

There is only one success—to be able to spend your life in your own way.
—Christopher Morley

DO WHAT YOU WANT

Mom used to say, "Jackie, you try harder than any kid I've ever seen." Usually, that was just her way of trying to make me feel better about not making the team or finishing in the middle of the pack at some competitive event. I might not have actually tried harder than any of the kids, but I sure did try hard when I wanted something.

Not always getting what I wanted probably turned out to be a good life lesson. Learning to get up and try again without taking it personally helped build stamina and success in my life. Mostly, those "failures" helped me identify my strengths. Along the road, different people and opportunities showed up, and I was fortunate enough to be awake when they did.

My first real memory of thinking differently was during my junior year of high school. All students were "requested" to sell $25 or more in raffle tickets in order to raise money for our school. I thought, *Here we go again . . . mom and dad, aunts, uncles, family friends, and neighbors forced to buy something they didn't want. Surely, there had to be a better way.*

I remember visiting with my math teacher, Brother Michael, about how we seemed to be doing the same thing over and over just to raise $25 per student. He looked at me with his full-toothed grin and said, "Do you have a better idea?" At that point, he and I talked about some different ways I might challenge the normal way of fund-raising. Little did I know then how important his words would be in helping me find my unique talent. What happened next surprised even me.

After school that day, I went to the accounting office and requested a list of every business that did work for our school. Remember, this was 1964, and no student in my school had ever asked for that kind of information. Of course, I was told no. I'm still not sure why I didn't just stop there, but something in my gut told me I was on to something. Finally, after taking my request all the way to the principal, I was given a list of companies who had been paid something by Bishop Kelley High School. Over the next three weeks, I contacted most of these companies in person and convinced each one to donate between $25 and $250 for raffle tickets. I simply did not take no for an answer, and I'm sure some coughed up the money just to get me to stop talking. Curiously enough, I was asked by several of the company owners to check back with them when I was ready to look for a job. This seemed like a very nice compliment for someone who had just barged into their front door, asking for money. I was the top fund-raiser for Bishop Kelley High School in 1964. Not only was I the top fund-raiser, I was spectacular! In hindsight, *spectacular* is a little overstated. But when you feel that good about success, it becomes an exclamation point in your life.

I'm good at being able to see things differently and dealing with all the people who say no. Like a dumb puppy wagging his tail after being shooed away, it's not your lack of ability to hear *no*; it's your ability to keep coming back.

Many things didn't go the way I'd planned or hoped. I didn't make the team most of the time. I rarely got the deal. I failed more often than not, I've been told no far more often than yes, and I've been fired from three sales jobs along the way.

It's funny how people can impact your life. At first, you may see actions that affect you only in the short term. Later, as you examine the direction your life has taken, you realize some individuals affected your core philosophy as well. Leonard Ritz Sr., who owned CFR prior to my purchase in 1986, is one of those people.

In 1979, I had just been fired from a sales job with an independent insurance broker. Leonard called and asked me to come see him. I had a unique talent, and he had a need for this talent in his company. Leonard had gone head-to-head against me in bidding two accounts that he ultimately won. My life might have taken a different turn had I gotten them because although I didn't get the accounts, I had made an impact on Leonard. (A good presentation might not get you the job, but you never know who will be paying attention). Leonard was so impressed with my presentation he offered me a job managing his biggest accounts. Over the next few years, I was able to grow that book of business to one of the most loyal and profitable client lists in the state. Ultimately, I purchased CFR, which has become one of the premier insurance brokerage firms in the United States. Sometimes great things happen to us when we least expect them.

This experience helped me develop one of my strongest beliefs in how to create successful opportunities for others. I believe when you help people discover their unique ability and give them the opportunity and tools to excel, you create an environment for success.

There is something inside you so strongly connected to your being that you simply cannot ignore it. It is not your intelligence, personality, emotional intellect, or learned behavior. It is your instinctive uniqueness that makes certain things you do seem natural.

Deep down, our instinct tells us we are unique, that we have capabilities yet to be drawn upon. I strongly believe your natural talent is a gift from your Creator, and you have a responsibility to share this gift with others.

Good stuff and bad stuff happens to all of us. I recommend a bad memory for the bad stuff and a good memory for the good stuff.

Enjoy the ride!

Jack Allen

KEY SUCCESS FACTORS: Passion, Determination, Faith

RECOMMENDED BOOKS: *First, Break All the Rules: What the World's Greatest Managers Do Differently* by Marcus Buckingham and Curt Coffman, *Follow This Path: How the World's Greatest Organizations Drive Growth by Unleashing Human Potential* by Curt Coffman, *Good to Great: Why Some Companies Make the Leap . . . and Others Don't* by Jim Collins, *Hero Z: Empower Yourself, Your Coworkers, Your Company* by William C. Byham with Jeff Cox, *Now, Discover Your Strengths* by Marcus Buckingham and Donald O. Clifton, *Play to Win! Choosing Growth Over Fear In Work and Life* by Larry Wilson, *Powered by Instinct: 5 Rules for Trusting Your Guts* by Kathy Kolbe, *The Fifth Discipline: The Art and Practice of the Learning Organization* by Peter M. Senge, *Who Moved My Cheese?: An Amazing Way to Deal With Change in Your Work and in Your Life by* Spencer Johnson, *Working With Emotional Intelligence* by Daniel Goleman, *TheTruth About You* by Marcus Buckingham

WEB SITES: *www.cfr-ins.com, www.whateveryyoudo.com*

EDITOR'S NOTES: Jack Allen Jr. is the Chief Executive Officer of Whatever You Do Inc. The company was formed with the mission of becoming a primary resource for products and information about management methodology, corporate culture, and corporate vision.

Jack is also the Chairman of CFR Inc., a large regional insurance brokerage firm specializing in providing corporate insurance products. He has successfully grown the company from a small local firm to one of the top privately owned insurance agencies in the United States. CFR was selected as one of the 2008 Best Places to Work in Oklahoma.

Jack has participated in many business programs such as the Disney University Leadership Course, Adizes Management Methodology Training, the Kolbe Corporation Executive Program, the Strategic Coach Program, the Sitkins 100 (1 percent-ers), and the Peter Senge Seminars. In addition, Jack has attended presentations and various workshops led by Tom Peters, Deepak Chopra, Ken Blanchard, Stephen Covey, Anthony Robins, Peter Drucker, Lee Iacocca, Harvey Mackay, Peter Ueberroth, Robert Waterman, and Marcus Buckingham. He regularly gives presentations on corporate vision and corporate culture to groups ranging from the advertising industry and insurance industry to a multitude of companies in the service industry.

Jack has been on the editorial advisory board for *Rough Notes* magazine and is a member of the Oklahoma State University Spears School of Business Hall of Fame. He was selected as one of the 25 Most Innovative Agents in America. He is an active participant in professional insurance organizations and holds board positions on several charitable, educational, and civic organizations.

You see things; and you say "Why?" But I dream things that never were; and I say "Why not?"
—George Bernard Shaw

TWO PHONE CALLS THAT CHANGED MY LIFE

As a young boy, I always watched the TV show *The Millionaire*. I used to imagine how it would feel to have a check for a million dollars in my hands and all the things I would do. Being a millionaire seemed like an impossible dream, but it was my dream, and I believed dreams could come true.

My first business venture came from hearing a song and having an idea. Christmas is always special, but to a nine-year-old, it is a truly magical time. As I listened to the song lyrics "I saw Mommy kissing Santa Claus underneath the mistletoe last night," I remembered seeing a huge amount of mistletoe in the park. I found my friend Joe and convinced him we could make a fortune selling mistletoe. We "borrowed" paper sacks from the movie theater, began filling them with mistletoe, and started selling door-to-door at fifty cents a bag. Most of the customers bought two bags, and we soon had almost one hundred dollars—enough money for the best Christmas ever! This first business venture encouraged me to believe in my dreams and not be afraid to try something new.

About ten years later, I had an idea that would change my life. My uncle had developed a catfish bait that smelled really bad; in fact, it stunk, so the name Little Stinker was quite accurate. Catfish loved the smell, and fishermen hated it—but they loved the results they got when they used the bait. We discussed different ways to package the bait and tried several alternatives. Genius has been described as 1 percent inspiration and 99 percent perspiration, and that was certainly our experience. I can't remember how many times we failed, but we kept trying. Then as I was visiting my mother one afternoon, I noticed a cluster of artificial grapes and had one of those eureka moments. I envisioned how the bait could be used without fishermen having to touch it. I still had lots of failures until I refined the design and created the mold, and thus Little Stinker was born. I convinced local TV personality Don Wallace to demo the product on his outdoors show, and suddenly the orders began to flow in; soon we had our first $100,000 in sales.

Having seen the power of TV advertising, I then approached a young fisherman named Jimmy Houston about sponsoring his TV show, and our sales soared to $1 million, thanks to Little Stinker's placement in Kmart and a few Wal-Mart stores. One Saturday morning, as I sat in my office, the phone rang, and the regional manager from Wal-Mart said Sam Walton would like to speak to me. Sam told me he was very impressed with our product and wanted to buy all of our production. This was really flattering and a great temptation, but I told Mr. Walton I could not in good conscience turn my back on those companies that had helped me succeed. He said he appreciated my honesty and integrity and asked if I could fill an order for all of his stores. I said I could, and he told me he would send a purchase order for $360,000. We had to work around the clock for two weeks to fill the order, but we did it.

The only motivational book I ever read was the Bible, and my business practice was based on the Golden Rule. Being true to the principles I learned from reading the Bible resulted in my largest order and set the stage for the second phone call that would make my childhood dream come true. After continuing to grow our sales, once again, the phone rang; and a business broker asked if I would be interested in selling my company. I had not even thought about the possibility of selling, but I agreed to sign a nondisclosure agreement and meet with the interested party at the upcoming trade show. At the show, I was shocked to meet the top executives from the Johnson Wax Company, who asked to fly down and visit our factory. A few weeks later, my wife, Linda, and I flew to Wisconsin and agreed to sell the company. On the flight back, I realized I had achieved my childhood dream of becoming a millionaire because I was holding a check for $1 million, and more would be coming.

Two phone calls changed my life, but they came because I dared to dream and never gave up on achieving my dream. It had taken eight years of countless struggles and frustrations, but patience, persistence and belief in my dream resulted in success. You too can achieve your dreams if you will plan your work and work your plan. As Winston Churchill once said, "Never, never, never, give up." We never quit following our dream, and we pray you won't give up on yours.

Rocky Marshall

KEY SUCCESS FACTORS: Confidence, Perseverance, Faith

RECOMMENDED BOOKS: The Bible

WEB SITE: *www.turbopowerenergy.com*

EDITOR'S NOTES: Rocky is CEO of Bio-Rite Nutritionals LLC. He and his wife, Linda, enjoy boating, fishing, and hunting and have five children and six grandchildren. For inspiration, they read the Bible and are actively involved in their church. Rocky also served as CEO and founder of a telecommunications company and is currently involved in a new product launch with Bio-Rite. Rocky is also available for speaking engagements.

There's only one way to succeed in anything and that is to give everything.
—*Vince Lombardi*

DOT-COM MILLIONAIRE BY AGE NINETEEN

When I read the stories of successful people, I frequently enjoy the overall tale. However, I often don't understand exactly how they got started and what specific actions they took to get things off the ground. That is always the hardest part and the most useful to learn when trying to achieve success for one's self. As such, I wanted my story to focus on the details of how I got started before moving on to other successes.

The date was the first of April 2003, and little did I know this day would eventually become one of the most significant in my entire life. I was fifteen, in school in England doing my GCSEs (essentially the UK version of SATs), and had just got a new Web site live. I had recently been having a lot of fun messing around with a program on my PC called Flash, which is basically an open storyboard allowing you to make digital animations. Being a bit of a joker, I was using the program to make funny animations of my friends at school—harmless things such as inside jokes of people falling over—and they became popular. Due to the limitations of Flash, I couldn't just e-mail the clips; I had to upload them to a Web site. HolyLemon.com was born. An odd name, for sure; it was inspired by one of the animations where a cat morphs into an angelic lemon, and back again. Many of the clips were slapstick and pretty bizarre, but seemed to be a style that worked.

With the site launching, I would be able to share my animations with everyone at my school and, I soon realized, the wider world. Traffic started off pretty low, perhaps ten or twenty visitors a day. I wanted to figure out a way of increasing the number. I learned about something called search engine optimization (SEO), which allows you to tweak your Web site so you rank high in the search results on sites like Google and Yahoo. I focused on the phrase "funny animations". I scoured the Web constantly for new resources and researched every last thing there was to know on SEO. Eventually, it paid off, as I began to rank highly, and the number of daily visitors crept up—thirty, forty, fifty, eighty, one hundred! At this point, I was totally hooked. *How high can I take this?* I asked myself. I had visions of thousands of people visiting the site each day. *What influence, what power!* I joked with my friends!

Around this time, I also began to experiment with trying to make money from the site. On the Web, there are a few key ways of making money from advertising—cost per thousand (CPM) ads, where you run banners and get paid per one thousand times they are seen; cost per click (CPC) ads, where you get paid per click; and cost per action (CPA) ads, where you make money every time someone buys something through your site. I experimented constantly with the different formats and discovered a mix of CPM and CPA advertising was optimal. As soon as I received my first check, it all became real—they actually did pay, and I was totally hooked on trying to see how much I could make (despite the first check being for only $10!).

I immediately set my sights on a higher goal: the number one ranking for the search results for "funny videos." I had recently decided to add a couple of funny videos to the Web site, and they had done extremely well—many more people came to see the videos than my animations (I could have been offended, but I wasn't—I just cared about increasing my traffic, and thus my revenue). After approximately five months of nonstop work, I managed to secure the top spot when "funny videos" was typed into Google, and it all snowballed from there.

All of a sudden, I was getting over ten thousand visitors a day, and through people telling their friends, the number crept up every day—eleven thousand, twelve thousand, fifteen thousand, eighteen thousand, twenty thousand.

It was emotionally a very polar experience. On the one hand, I was totally elated. I had done it; I had gotten to the top spot and was getting lots of visitors! I had won, and it felt great. But at the same time, I was looking at my costs, and as videos cost a lot more to host on a Web site than animations, my costs were skyrocketing too. Serving over 3 million videos that month (on average fifteen thousand people per day watching five videos each per visit) meant I was going to get a hosting bill for $5,000 that month, when the site only made $1,000! I had to go into advertising overdrive and spent the next week running nonstop experiments to try to figure out how to bring the revenue up to at least match the costs. Eventually, through trial and error, I figured it out, and the site began making a lot of money every month. I worked on making it better and better, and popularity kept climbing, eventually reaching over 150,000 people every single day.

After a couple of years of running HolyLemon throughout high school and my first year of university, I received an offer to sell from a company called LiveUniverse, the brainchild of MySpace cofounder Brad Greenspan. Greenspan had left MySpace at this point, taken the $40 million he made from selling it, and set up his next businesses. While I was excited to discuss the possibility of exiting, I felt the figures undervalued the business and was pleased when I got a higher counteroffer from another company that had expressed an interest in acquiring the business. This company, HandHeld Entertainment, was listed on the NASDAQ stock exchange. After numerous trips between the UK and California (where they were based), we ended up agreeing on a sale price of $1.25 million to be made up of a mixture of cash, shares, and earn out (being paid based on further success of the site). I was extremely happy; it was a very surreal experience, especially as the deal had almost fallen through a number of times. And so as well as being happy, I was also slightly relieved. The University of Bath (where I was currently studying) put out a press release for the sale when I returned, and I had the most bizarre few days of my entire life. I was interviewed for ten radio stations, five print newspapers, seven news Web sites, and three news agencies, and even made it on the national TV news. A very intense few days, to say the least!

The primary reason April 1, 2003, was such a significant day for me was not because it sparked a chain of events that led to making lots of money or being in the newspaper, but because it led me to discover what I really enjoy in life—entrepreneurship and starting companies. I am so grateful for the experience because it taught me at a young age what I truly enjoy; and for that reason, I'll never work a day in my life, as the old saying goes.

Beyond HolyLemon, I have also cofounded a video games news and reviews Web site, PlayStation Universe, *www.psu.com*, which is read by over 1 million gamers a month. I cofounded it with Seb Hayes, a school friend; and we initially grew it with SEO and then sustained the growth with quality editorials. We employ mostly college students on a part-time basis and pay them per article they write, with full-time editors who ensure the work is up to par. As well as the main site, PSU also has a forum community, *www.ps3forums.com*, with over 150,000 gamers on the site. These two sites are profitable from selling advertising to big game companies. I started this site when I was sixteen, about a year after I founded HolyLemon, and was able to run them simultaneously by outsourcing all of the time-consuming tasks to third-party freelancers.

In my penultimate year of university, Seb and I had the idea of creating a social networking Web site for gamers. The more we thought about it, the more we couldn't ignore how popular and fun it could become. We decided to quit university and work full-time on building this vision. We partnered with Ben Phillips, an extremely talented software developer I knew from an internship I'd completed at an online advertising network. The three of us cofounded Playfire.com in Soho, the exciting media district of London. We raised $1 million in seed funding from a number of high-profile angel investors (including Michael Birch, the founder of Bebo; and Chris Deering, the former CEO of PlayStation). As I write this, I am working 24/7 to make Playfire a success, just as I did for HolyLemon and PSU. Only time will tell if it takes off, but we are having a lot fun building this company, and at the end of the day, that's what counts.

Kieran O'Neill

KEY SUCCESS FACTORS: Experimentation, Passion, Effort, Constant Learning

RECOMMENDED BOOKS: *Purple Cow* by Seth Godin (the most important book on branding and marketing—and it's short too!), *Think and Grow Rich* by Napoleon Hill, *How to Win Friends and Influence People* by Dale Carnegie, *How to Get Rich* by Felix Dennis

WEB SITE: *www.holylemon.com, www.psu.com, www.playfire.com*

EDITOR'S NOTES: Kieran is working full-time as CEO of Playfire, the social network for video game players he cofounded alongside Seb Hayes and Ben Phillips in December 2007. PlayStation Universe (www.psu.com), a premium content destination and community for video game players and one of three companies cofounded by Kieran, is currently read by over 1 million gamers per month. The forum community, *www.ps3forums.com*, has over 3 million posts and circa 150,000 members. Kieran O'Neill was the winner of the 2008 Global Student Entrepreneur Awards UK and was the Chairman of BANTER (Bath Entrepreneur Society) at the University of Bath.

Opportunity dances with those who are ready on the dance floor.
—*H. Jackson Brown Jr.*

SUCCESS COMES WITH RESPONSIBILITY

As a rather poor family in Colorado, we never had a whole lot of opportunities, but we were always taught to work for what we had and be thankful for what we got. Unlike a lot of kids today, we were forced to find things to do, like building our own tree house or using inner tubes to build makeshift rafts that we used to fish with in the local irrigation canal. After we moved to Oregon, we eventually started to have a better life; but even then, we always had to work around the house or do yard work if we wanted to earn some extra money.

As I entered high school and got my driver's license, I began to work after school. My first job was as a cleaner at a small local custom meat-packing company. This job was anything but glamorous, but it made me enough money to put gas in my old truck and have a little left over for the girls. After that, I worked for a tire company, and then an auto-parts store—all before I graduated from high school. I always earned decent grades in high school and planned on going to college to pursue a degree in veterinary medicine.

After high school, I went to college at Eastern Oregon University. It took me only two semesters to realize college wasn't for me. I headed back to my hometown of Eugene, Oregon, where I joined the Army National Guard and started working for Morse Brothers Inc. as a manual laborer building forms for giant concrete bridge beams. Morse Brothers was a good company, and I made decent money; but the work was hard, wet, and sometimes very cold. I knew there was more to life than what I was doing. After seven years there, I decided it was time to pursue other avenues of employment.

I bought an online real estate licensing exam, which prepared me to take the Oregon State real estate exam, which I passed the first go-around. At this time, I was living in a small town named Harrisburg, just outside of Eugene. There was a new real estate office in town called Allstate Real Estate. I stopped in one day after work and asked the owner if he could use any part-time real estate agents. At the time, he didn't have any other agents working for him, so he gave me a desk and said with a chuckle, "Go get 'em, tiger." With those words, I became very motivated to start my new career. In the beginning, I worked my regular job and worked real estate in the afternoons, evenings, and every weekend I could. It was hard in the beginning. I had to use my own money, and I had a hard time selling a single home. The greatest milestone in any real estate professional's career is the sale of their first home. June 25, 2004, was my milestone. After that first sale, I knew I had what it took to become successful in this industry.

Following the sale of my first home, I quit my job and started working real estate full-time. I would sell or list a house for everyone I knew—friends, family, and coworkers. During this time, I did everything I could to better myself including reading, listening to tapes, and attending seminars. At the end of my first year with Allstate, I was named Agent of the Year and Rookie of the Year, and had accounted for nearly 65 percent of everything made out of that office.

Working for Allstate helped me to really get a solid foot in the door, as well as gave me some concrete experience. Then the opportunity came to move on to Keller Williams Realty, where I had over $3 million in sales during the next year. Along the way, I built some very strong relationships with people in the industry. Relationships are very important and can make your business prosper if they are used correctly. I learned to be ethical in everything I do. Sometimes money can be made by taking shortcuts that will catch up with you negatively in the long run.

Two years with Keller Williams enabled me to build strong business relationships and gain in-depth knowledge of the real estate industry and, most importantly, gave me the opportunity to build up a nice cash flow. This led to my next business venture, an opportunity to run my own real estate franchise by buying into a Century 21 franchise for $30,000. I was at the top of my game, the real estate industry in the Pacific Northwest was booming, and I now had my own company. But after three months with Century 21, I happened on a bill that had been left unpaid. Up to this point, I hadn't had an active role in the company's finances. After inquiring about the bill I had received, I started looking over the company's financials and found something very disturbing: the partners were skimming the company's resources to pay for personal luxuries.

Buying into the franchise became a very expensive business lesson. I knew the company didn't have a chance of surviving, so I took a $30,000 loss and left. I lost virtually everything I had, and on top of that, the subprime mortgage mess had just begun. So I packed up and went back to the real estate office where I had started. I arranged to buy the office with my last $2,000 and the title to my old Chevy pickup; from there, I was able to start rebuilding.

Though the market has been tough, I now own three real estate offices and have over thirty agents who work for my group. I have learned many lessons along the way, with the most important being, always take an active role in your company's finances because in the end, the entrepreneur is ultimately responsible.

Success is a wonderful thing and can come with great responsibility. I believe in giving back to the community as much as possible. Doing so not only makes me feel wonderful, it helps my business grow in the long run. I personally am a member of the local volunteer fire department and donate time and money to various local charities. I realize many organizations are not financially strong enough to make donations, but they can make up for that through donation of time.

If there is one thing I truly regret, it is not finishing school the first time around. I learned through trial and error, education is very important. With formal business training, the $30,000 loss I experienced would have never happened. This is why I decided to go back to school and pursue my degree in business, which is complemented by experience in my industry.

I try as often as possible to read and educate myself. I believe it is important to gain a perspective on life from outside sources, and what better way than through books. Even if people do not consider themselves entrepreneurs, it is vital they educate themselves as much as possible so they can run their own lives to their utmost potential.

Joe Alcorn
Contributed by Stevan J. Alcorn

KEY SUCCESS FACTORS: Honesty, Relationships, Education, Ethics, Giving Back

RECOMMENDED BOOKS: *Rich Dad Poor Dad* by Robert T. Kiyosaki, *The Millionaire Next Door* by Thomas J. Stanley and William D. Danko, *Today's the Day* by Jim Stovall

WEB SITE: *www.joealcorn.net*

EDITOR'S NOTES: Joe Alcorn currently lives in Harrisburg, Oregon, and owns three real estate offices.

CHAPTER FIVE

NETWORKING AND RELATIONSHIPS

Make a habit of dominating the listening and let the customer dominate the talking.
—*Brian Tracy*

Today knowledge has power. It controls access to opportunity and advancement.
—Peter F. Drucker

ENTREPRENEURSHIP IN THE TWENTY-FIRST CENTURY

Recently celebrating my ninety-fourth birthday, I am still happily involved in entrepreneurial ventures. I have been an entrepreneur since 1954, when I decided to bite the bullet and introduce the first woman-owned commercial travel agency in the very competitive market of New York City. Everyone said it was a foolish move and if I wished to open a travel agency, it should be the traditional agency, which handled personal travel, rather than commercial. Now I was competing with the big boys, including American Express and Thomas Cook. Every obstacle seemed to be put in my way. The only lease I could get for office space was in a building that needed renovation, and the owners were so positive I would be out of business in six months that this was the lease they offered me. Airlines and cruise companies refused to send ticket stock to my office, and banks were most reluctant to lend me money, which would have made my life much easier.

However, I decided to invest the small amount of capital I had in advertising. I had my agency print up a very attractive brochure outlining the special services we would be rendering to our clients. I then spent days going to local office buildings and dropping off my brochures with the receptionists, along with a red rose. Sure enough, I attracted a public relations firm, which was not a very lucrative client. However, since this firm had the Pepsi-Cola account worldwide, I took exceptionally good care of its travelers, hoping they would introduce me into the Pepsi-Cola world. Sure enough, Mr. Relin called me one day to say Alfred Steele, chairman of the Pepsi-Cola Company, and his new bride, the famous movie star Joan Crawford, were endeavoring to obtain accommodations on the new ship the SS *United States*. Although I was not an agent for Pepsi-Cola, I spent the mornings of the next few weeks at the U.S. Line, anxiously awaiting a cancellation of one of the five luxury suites, in which Mr. Steele was interested.

One day a customer who was holding a suite, which was not quite as luxurious as the five I was interested in, cancelled. I asked for a one-day option on that suite. The U.S. bookers were not aware that while I had been visiting them, I had looked over their booking charts and taken down the names and phone numbers of the people who were holding reservations on the five luxury suites. I called one of them, a man in Wyoming, and told him my problem; I said if he would make a switch with me for the suite I now had an option on, I would pay for his trip (a very small investment for the possibility of capturing the Pepsi-Cola account). The gentleman immediately told me if he could be introduced to Joan Crawford, he would agree to relinquish. When I went to see Mr. Steele, he said, "Young lady, tell me how you stole that suite from my travel department and Columbia Pictures, Joan Crawford's agency." When I explained to him what I had done, he laughed, called in his secretary, and gave me a letter, which said I now had the Pepsi-Cola account worldwide! Joan Crawford became not only my client but a very special friend who brought me several national accounts.

Suddenly my landlord and suppliers were beating a path to my door. In the next ten years, my agency became one of the most successful in Manhattan. I finally sold it when my husband's company asked us to come to Chicago for two years. Unfortunately, the new owner did not render the personal service we had given these very important clients, and he was soon forced to close the agency.

In Chicago, I now decided it was payback time. So I volunteered to teach a travel course at a girl's reformatory. I loved working with these troubled young women and was extremely successful in getting them interested in studying for the first time in their lives. When they were about to graduate, I pleaded with United Airlines to take the girls on a one-hour flight over the city, during which they would be served lunch and receive their diplomas. I felt this would motivate them toward a travel career.

When we arrived at the airport, I was shocked by the amount of press coverage United Airlines had attracted. As a result, I began receiving inquiries from all across the United States, asking where they could enroll in my travel course. This led me, with the help of my brilliant husband, to open Echols International Travel School here in Chicago. At the time, there were no travel schools in America. This venture turned out to be enormously successful over the next thirty-five years, with branches being opened in other cities.

The National Association of Women Business Owners of both New York and Chicago in 1985 voted me the Entrepreneur of the Year.

I truly believe this era is the perfect time for young people to consider an entrepreneur venture, providing they have something to offer in which the public is interested. Being in charge of your own destiny is a wonderful challenge for the ambitious young person who has complete confidence in his/her capability.

Evelyn Echols

KEY SUCCESS FACTORS: Taking Initiative, Acting on Opportunity, Confidence

RECOMMENDED BOOK: *They Said I Couldn't Do It, But I Did* by Evelyn Echols

WEB SITE: *www.evelynechols.com*

EDITOR'S NOTE: Ms. Evelyn Echols is a member of the CEO Entrepreneurship Hall of Fame and currently conducts a lecture series on entrepreneurship at major universities across the country. She has received awards from many foreign countries for her work in creating goodwill among nations through the medium of travel. She has just released her second published book, *They Said I Couldn't Do It, But I Did.*

One of our greatest gifts is our intuition. It is a sixth sense we all have—we just need to learn to tap into and trust it.

—Donna Karan

I WAS BORN WITH A GIFT

All my life, I have found people are drawn to me, seeking knowledge to improve their life path. I, in turn, am passionately devoted to my clients. For the past seventeen years, I have been setting up a table on the oceanfront to counsel people about their lives. Many times, those who see me on the Venice Beach boardwalk say they chose me because I was the only one who looked like a true psychic.

A lot of people are not as strongly psychic as I am. Psychic abilities are passed through bloodlines, and I am fortunate to have European parents. My mother was French, and my father was German/Welsh. I'm eccentric, sweet, kind, very loving, strong-willed, and determined.

When I was two years old, I loved listening to a scary mystery program on the radio (television was just being developed) called *The Shadow*. It was on weekdays only in the afternoon. At exactly the right time each day before the program began, I would pull my little red chair up to the radio and quietly sit, waiting for my mother to turn it on. I never said a word. I would just wait for her. She would see me sitting there, turn on the radio, and tune it to the correct station. I would always know when the program started and would hear the opening words, "The shadow knows." When I was four, my parents traveled to Belgium, where they took me to a university to have my psychic abilities tested. I passed with flying colors! I am not only psychic but also intuitive, empathic, and clairvoyant. My parents were given a certified document stating I am a natural-born psychic. In the United States, no one tests for psychic abilities, so almost anyone can call themselves a psychic.

I always knew things other children at school did not know. I knew if we were having chocolate or regular milk, cookies or cupcakes, substitute teachers, assemblies, or surprise tests. It amazed me others did not know these things, but at home, it was treated as nothing unusual and quite normal. As I grew older, I began to realize I did have special gifts.

I have always shared my gifts with others. Although I thought I would wait until I was old and would sit in my rocking chair and read palms and tarot on the Venice Beach boardwalk, all of this changed in 1992. I was a corporate executive working in the management information systems (MIS) profession and had just successfully completed a system that was up and running smoothly. In 1992, corporations were instructed to tighten their belts—this translated into downsizing. One person out of four was the usual attrition rate. I fell into that equation.

After being a model, a clothing manufacturer, and a member of the corporate world, I decided to use my gift and make my living being a psychic. With no new systems to develop, I made my way down to the Venice Beach boardwalk to check out the competition. I selected three psychics at random to see what I was up against. The first gentleman was a smooth talker and quite good-looking. He took a brief look at my palm and said, "You're a cute little thing—you should do very well on the boardwalk." (So much for a psychic reading!) He later left the beach and became an evangelist. My second reading was by an English gentleman, who was quite a snappy dresser. He did a little of everything from tarot cards, palms, and crystals to diving. His readings were not very accurate, but he put on a good show. After a while, he asked me if what he was saying was anywhere close to the truth. I replied no. He told me to keep my money. The third psychic was older, seasoned. I had finally hit the jackpot. He called himself the Wizard and definitely looked the part. He read my palm, and I was totally impressed. He was excellent and later helped me fine-tune my own palmistry readings. He taught me many of the incredible and countless variations of palm readings. I asked him if he did tarot readings, and he exclaimed, "No way!" He said reading tarot was just too complicated, and it was too much trouble trying to remember all of the various meanings to each card and their placement. He said, "Give me a nice palm any old day."

I felt very good about my competition since the Wizard did not do tarot card readings. I designed a killer sign, and one in which no other sign on the boardwalk could compete. Next, I needed to find a place for my business and decide whether to use Persian prayer pillows or a table and chairs. Chairs and a draped table covered in crystals and crystal balls won out. It proved much more professional and comfortable to ask clients to sit in a chair than on the ground. I have certain crystals to keep away evil spirits. Sometimes crazy people come into my space, but I do a special clearing of my mind, creating circles of light. Dark can't stand light, so they go away. Even if they are standing in front of me and trying to block me, I don't have to tell them to go away; they just do.

The more I use my psychic powers, the stronger I have become. I experience dreams or visions that come true and am also able to speak to people who have passed over. This is very comforting to the people left behind, for many have unanswered questions. I am able to make this connection and give them answers they are desperately seeking.

Once, I had a dream/vision about a person who worked at the hair salon where I have my hair styled. Although I was never close to this person, we have always been on a friendly basis. I dreamed she would very soon meet her future husband at a very exciting place involving horses. She said, "Great!" She needed to meet a good man, and she was riding in a rodeo that weekend. I told her to keep her eyes and ears open. She met a man at the rodeo and brought him to the salon for me to see. I took one look and said, "That's the very same man I saw in my dream." They married about a year later and now live happily on a ranch in California where they raise horses.

Often, I predict the sex of a baby, and I am always right. A couple who came to me was having a tough time getting pregnant. It wasn't happening! I told them the month they were going to get pregnant and that it was going to be a baby girl. It just came to me—I don't know where or how, but the name was Sierra. Fourteen months later, they came up to me and showed me their baby daughter, who was born in October (the month I predicted), and they had named her Sierra. That was nice!

One day, on my way to the beach, I stopped at a local corner store. As I was leaving, I heard the words, "Oh my god, it's her." A woman across the street was yelling, "She's the one," and waving her arms wildly over her head. I thought to myself, *What have I done now?* I had given this woman a tarot card reading on the beach. I had told her she should soon end her unhappy marriage and predicted she would meet the man of her dreams, remarry, and be incredibly happy in her new life. She said, "Fat chance." She worked in Tokyo teaching children how to speak English and told me that the people at the school and surrounding area were all Asians. For her to meet someone was almost an impossibility. Now she was saying I was totally amazing and then introduced me to her new husband. The chances of my prediction becoming true were next to nothing, yet it had all happened. She was so happy she had found me to tell me of this miracle.

People approach me all the time to tell me everything I predicted has come true. I read a gentleman's palm one day, and although he was not in the best financial position at the time, I told him within five years, he was to come into a substantial amount of money. He returned to me five years later to thank me and said he had indeed been part of a lotto winning and his finances had greatly improved.

I feel my very special psychic gifts are paramount in my success as a psychic. I truly care about the happiness and success of my clients, regardless of their situation. Not all questions have the same answers. I am a relationship specialist and have a vast knowledge as to the working of the universe. This, plus a kind heart and a white aura that keeps negative people away from me, are the cornerstones to my success.

My philosophy is that everything has a time and reason. We don't always want to wait—we want things now, but it may not be our time. As far as I know, God is never late.

Luann Y. Hughes

KEY SUCCESS FACTORS: Relationships, Passion, Perseverance

RECOMMENDED BOOKS: *Tarot* by Eden Gray, *Fantasy Land* by Marc Lo Porto

EDITOR'S NOTES: Luann Hughes has been featured in at least four books about psychics and the Venice Beach boardwalk. She has been in several movies and various commercials. Ms. Hughes advertises internationally and would like to have her own psychic television show. She plans to write a book, which would help others with their relationships and understanding of the opposite sex.

Alone we can do so little; together we can do so much.
—Helen Keller

MY WILLFUL ENDEAVOR

Nothing will dampen the value of entrepreneurial freedom. I started my career after college by selling life insurance, and that taught me one great lesson—the value of freedom. Being an employee in the insurance business made me realize I did not want to work for someone else. It inspired me to develop my dream of owning my own business, to seize the opportunity when it came along. My first journey in business was starting a bus company in my hometown, Wichita, Kansas. After twenty years of success in my first business venture, another opportunity revealed itself. I wanted to get my son Alex a special baseball bat that I could only find online. However, in 1997, buying products online was not an option. I have always had a genuine interest in the development of the Internet and I saw an opportunity to build a retail store online. My other big interest is golf; consequently, the idea of the Golf Warehouse was born.

The demand for products online was escalating with the increased development and use of the Internet. I recognized the opportunity before most in the golf business, and I was determined to proceed with my ideas. Recognizing an opportunity is only the tip of the iceberg; the following years were filled with long workdays requiring exceptional determination and competitiveness. In October 1997, I contracted with a company to create a Web site. In April 1998, the first product was sold online and by the end of 1998, sales reached $1 million.

Especially in the beginning of the business, the workdays were extremely long. I had to have the full support from my family to proceed with my plan. As an entrepreneur, you are responsible for getting the work done, and there is plenty of hard work involved with producing a successful company. Another challenge is the varied skill set starting a business demands. You should be willing to do any task the business requires. You also need a family situation that allows for the risks and costs associated with being an entrepreneur. I recommend start-up capital to cover at least two years of expenses, since building repetitive customer relationships takes time. My first business, the bus company, was started with $30,000, and the initial capital for Golf Warehouse was $1 million.

The golf business is a challenge because of the relatively small target market. Twenty-eight million people in the United States play golf, but only 9 million are responsible for 85 percent of the money spent on equipment, green fees, membership dues, and apparel. The retail community is also challenging because there are approximately fifteen thousand green-grass pro shops selling golf equipment in addition to the thousands of off-course golf stores. Five major vendors cover 85-90 percent of sales: Titleist, Ping, Callaway, Nike, and TaylorMade/Adidas. The Golf Warehouse depends on those five vendors to supply its equipment, so the relationships with them are crucial. One of the most important elements of business and entrepreneurship is building good, long-term relationships.

In March of 2000, the dot-com fall created an enormous threat to our business. We reorganized to weather the storm and went into survival mode in order to keep the business going. Conserving capital became essential to the survival of the company. Business is very much like sport; no excuse will save you from not performing. You need to stay competitive and constantly focus on performance. I have not perceived any challenges in our business as threats because I have never feared failure. I have focused on being conservative with the use of capital, and I have been smart when it comes to adapting to the market. There is no need for me to fear failure. You need to have a realistic view and need to be flexible handling your business. As long as you have a strong work ethic and are willing to live with the risk, there is no downside to entrepreneurship. Entrepreneurship brings great freedom and opportunity for success.

A concern for the Golf Warehouse has been the recent decline in the stock market. By keeping a conservative use of capital, along with flexibility, we should be in good shape compared to many other retail golf operations that are saddled with large brick-and-mortar overhead.

Right from the beginning in 1998, the Golf Warehouse has flourished, and we were always profitable. In 1999, the Golf Warehouse was approached by IMG Sports Capital, which resulted in their investing in 70 percent of the company. The sale added reputational value, and in 2003, IMG sold its part of the firm to Sportsman's Guide, which added capital to the company. In 2005, the Golf Warehouse was sold to the European distribution company PPR. Catalogues were added to the business, and baseball equipment was added to the product line. There are also ideas about expanding into other sports, such as tennis.

The Golf Warehouse gives back to the community and others by offering good service. By taking care of business, we build long-term customer relationships, and this enables us to create job security for our staff, good benefits, and a pleasant work environment. Our main focus is to stay competitive, ensure customer service, and provide employee benefits. Additionally, the Golf Warehouse sponsors many charity golf tournaments and is actively involved in PPR initiatives such as the premier of the upcoming movie *Home,* which deals with the environmental challenges facing our planet.

There have been many successes throughout the history of the Golf Warehouse. Because of all the hard work, there has not been time to relish our victories. As an entrepreneur, you are always responsible. It is the thrill of the chase, and especially the building process, that makes it worthwhile. "Success is a journey, not a destination; the doing is often more important than the outcome."—Arthur Ashe

Most of the lessons I have learned are from developing the transportation business, and those were very valuable to me in the development of Golf Warehouse. First, the plan for a business has to be well thought through and realistic. Second, a conservative use of capital is very important; never get into too much debt. With the Golf Warehouse, we have never had debt. Keeping cash flows moving is vital, especially in the beginning of a business. It is important to not be tempted in the beginning to expand too fast because that could lead to an early failure. Also, making sure to have enough initial capital is critical. Third, customer satisfaction is crucial when starting up a new business.

Several personal characteristics are preferable if you are an entrepreneur. Being risk tolerant is important, as well as being flexible with the business. And being willing to adapt to changes in the market is vital in order to succeed. Also, as an entrepreneur, you need to be competitive and passionate about what you do. I often say entrepreneurs pay a very high price for their freedom—the price of long hours of hard work.

Mark Marney
Contributed by Karin Kinnerud

KEY SUCCESS FACTORS: Determination, Conservative Use of Capital, Customer Satisfaction

RECOMMENDED BOOKS: *They Call Me Coach* by John Wooden

WEB SITE: *www.tgw.com*

EDITOR'S NOTES: In 1976, Mr. Marney graduated from Oklahoma State University. Two years after graduation, he started his first business—a bus business in Wichita, Kansas, which was a success. In 1997, he started the Golf Warehouse, which has had continued success. The company was sold in 1999 to IMG Sports Capital. In 2003, it was sold to the Sportsman's Guide; and from 2005 until today, the Golf Warehouse has been owned by PPR, a European large-scale distributor.

Mr. Marney lives in Wichita, Kansas with his wife and daughter. He has two sons, one working for the Golf Warehouse and the other a student at Oklahoma State University. Mr. Marney has continued being involved in the Golf Warehouse, but he also has plans to start a new drop-ship business with his oldest son. The plan is to develop a marketing company that will use drop-shipping to eliminate the costs associated with excess handling of products between warehouses. Mr. Marney's target is to have 2 million different products online within three years.

Mr. Marney is also highly involved in the Magdalen Catholic Church, to which he contributes his monthly tithe, as well as other donations.

The nice thing about teamwork is that you always have others on your side.

—*Margaret Carty*

ENJOYING LIFE!

I always aspired to run my own business—to enjoy the freedom, to experience the feel of success, and to be able to see the fruits of my labor. Working in the hotel business proved to be very interesting and contributed to my success as an entrepreneur, but success didn't come to me overnight.

After college, I was interviewed to become one of the Marriott family members. Marriott had one position to be filled, and my friends from college were also applying. Starting a new chapter in my life straight out of college, I got on a plane and flew to New York City to interview for my first real professional job. Once I got to the hotel in New York City, I was focused and determined to compete for this job. Keep in mind the Marriott family is a very creative hotel chain, so I knew this was not going to be just a normal interview. When my girlfriends and I checked in to our individual rooms, there was a twelve-pack of beer in each room. Little did we know it was a test to find out who would and who wouldn't drink the beer in our rooms. I was the only one who didn't drink the beer and I got the job.

Being part of the Marriott family was not easy at first. Marriott puts its employees through intensive training. I was on a training program for one year, and within that year, I had to work in every department of the hotel. I started off in the kitchen, peeling carrots and cleaning dishes, thinking, *I have a degree, and I am peeling carrots and washing dishes.* I overcame my thoughts and decided this was another step in really getting the feel for each department. Eventually, I was the dishwasher's boss; and one by one, I learned the individual departments to finally become the general manager of the hotel. I never really entirely understood *teamwork* growing up because the only sport I played was tennis; but after a year, I was officially a member of the Marriott family.

After making a name for myself over the years at the Marriott, Sheraton Hotels made me a better offer. I moved to Florida where I met my husband. I had many years and lots of great and not-so-great experiences mastering the techniques of customer service. I realized, following the birth of my first child, and with another one on the way, that I wanted to have a more flexible job and be able to enjoy my family. Putting in fifty hours a week and being married to the hotel was not going to work for me in the future.

In 1999, while on maternity leave with my second child, I seized the opportunity to get my business with HelmsBriscoe off the ground. I felt I had the passion and knowledge to make my business in the meeting industry a big success. What does HelmsBriscoe do, you may ask? We leverage our experiences of more than nine hundred associates spanning thirty-six countries to deliver world-class solutions in the meeting industry. The collective knowledge shared among our seasoned associates is beyond comparison. Our process gives meeting planners back valuable time to plan their company's meetings or events. With the strength of the most trusted and largest site-selection firm in the world behind meeting planners, we leverage our power to negotiate better prices and better accommodations for our clients.

With so much excitement to get my own business off the ground, I started to master the technique of cold-calling companies to get the word out about HelmsBriscoe. Although I was determined to make this dream a reality, the first years were tough. At first, most companies I talked to already had their events planned for eight to eleven months out. Follow-up and building relationships with clients turned out to be key components to my success. Throughout the previous years of being in the hospitality business, I had built great relationships with other employees from different hotel chains. These relationships helped me negotiate better rates for my customers. My family and my competitiveness motivated me to do better and to be the best.

All the many challenges I have faced in my life have taught me lessons. An optimistic mind-set throughout life has enabled me to turn my failures into successes while learning what works and what doesn't work. Time management has also been a key component for me and has prompted me to ask myself, "Does this follow my business plan and fall within my core values?" Flexibility and adaptation are also important to me as an entrepreneur. With the economy being down and the travel industry also being down, I have really had to adapt to my surroundings quickly. Hard work and dedication to always do better have helped to increase my company's earnings by 20 percent over the last several years.

I have the passion to travel and plan huge successful events or meetings for different companies around the world. As I train new HelmsBriscoe associates and sit on the board as President of Meeting Professionals International, I really enjoy life and look forward to life's further adventures.

Cheryl Schreiner
Contributed by Adam Williams

KEY SUCCESS FACTORS: Relationships, Customer Service, Perseverance, Optimism, Work Ethic, Time Management

RECOMMENDED BOOKS: *A New Earth: Awakening to Your Life's Purpose* by Eckhart Tolle, *Green to Gold* by Daniel C. Esty and Andrew S. Winston, *The Accidental Millionaire* by Stephanie Frank

WEB SITE: *www.helmsbriscoe.com*

EDITOR'S NOTES: Cheryl Schreiner has a degree in hospitality from the University of Nevada and an MBA from Nova Southeastern University. Within two years of working, Cheryl brought at least $1 million in sales to HelmsBriscoe and still exceeds that number while having a job that works around her family. Cheryl serves as President of the Meeting Professionals International for the Northeast Florida chapter, the meeting and event industry's largest global community with twenty-four thousand members and sixty-nine chapters and clubs worldwide. Cheryl lives in Florida with her two children and her husband, who is now the food-and-beverage manager for Embassy Suites in Jacksonville.

You are a living magnet. What you attract into your life is in harmony with your dominant thoughts.
—*Brian Tracy*

THE HOT MOMMAS® PROJECT—NEED I SAY MORE?

Hot Mommas!!

- Laura Lee—A Fortune 500 golden girl gone entrepreneur. How did she do it? Did she have to give up her triathlon hobby? It had always helped her balance it all.
- Kimberly—A writer, podcaster, blogger, and clothing-line designer. All of these talents fell under one topic—yoga. She had three studios. Could she manage their growth with her constant flow of ideas for new ventures?
- Susan—Organized from birth. Susan ran the nation's largest radio PR firm. She had one child. Life was great. Then she learned twins were on the way. Life was about to get interesting.

And so it began . . . the Hot Mommas® Project.

The idea first came to me in the 1990s when I studied under Myra Hart at Harvard Business School. The project actually came into existence in 2002 when a bunch of kids at a Boys and Girls Club in Southeast Washington DC really put me over the edge. As I spoke to The National Foundation for Teaching Entrepreneurship students about these amazing women, I struck a nerve. "More!" the students told me. People were *intrigued*—these women "did it all."

But how did they do it? I started surveying Hot Mommas—how did they negotiate their personal and professional lives when they had high expectations for both? I pored over their responses to the survey I sent out: fortitude, flexibility . . . . Less respectable *F* words littered *my* brain when I tried to "do it all." I began to take notes. The notes turned into case studies (a fancy term for stories used in classrooms). I used the case studies in my class at the George Washington University, where I taught part-time.

The personal and the professional intertwined. This was real life. This represented the entrepreneurs I knew. Why weren't we hearing about them? The Hot Mommas® Project had tapped into this need. It spread like wildfire. We were producing role models on paper for women, girls, and students of business and life everywhere. I wanted to see these role models in classrooms.

"I've got a Hot Momma for you!" I heard several times a day. I could never write all these cases; students and other women around the world would never know their stories. But I felt responsible, so it was time to kick it into high gear.

I approached software developer FMS Inc. about building a case wizard software, which would take everyday people through the process of writing their own cases. Most of the software development cost was underwritten by Linda Rabbitt, supermega entrepreneur, CEO of Rand Construction, and a generous donor to the George Washington University School of Business. And our venture, housed at the university, was consistent with its support of women leaders. The rest of the funding? I scraped it together from my own bank account.

Those "scrapings" would have helped my family; it would have paid our mortgage. Turning that money over to a software vendor was hard. I had to leave behind the financially conservative person I had been. It was a completely different way of thinking for me—investing to create something bigger. "This ain't no carry-on luggage," I say about baggage that accompanies heavy issues like money. But I put on my big-girl undies and got through that mental battle. I told myself it was worth it and tried really hard to believe it, especially when the bank account said $0.00.

People need to know the idea is there. It's like that "if a tree falls in a forest" riddle. We were invited into a new world—the world of social media—by Guy Kawasaki (whom I consider the fairy godfather of social media) and we *crushed* it. We attended conferences, we met bloggers, we got on Twitter, we got on Facebook, and we sent questions out to LinkedIn. We had built the Case Wizard and they better come. We held a case competition to encourage people to write their cases. It worked. People found out about us. They liked us. News stories were done on us. More people found out about us.

We had a secret weapon—credibility. No matter how silly the name, *the Hot Mommas® Project* grew some serious teeth when we became the darlings of academia. Of course, we had tested the name. But in the early days, when I was writing all the cases,

I had expected a full-on rejection with a name like *Hot Mommas*. On the contrary, we were one of three national winners of a Coleman Foundation Case Award. The cases were published in one of Pearson Prentice Hall's top textbooks. The embrace of the academic community just keeps coming. So, folks, we can all be proud of our higher education teachers. They get it. We topped that off with a great research-based mission and an absolutely *killer* panel of judges, which we acquired through relationships, which gets me to the next point.

"You need good people!" I'd always hear people say. It was so annoying. How did I know how to find them, or even know when I had someone good? Here's the answer: *trust me, you know.* All of a sudden, things are getting done faster, better. This person makes your life easier. You find yourself semi-daydreaming about this person and how to clone them and fearing the day they will leave. That is how you know how you have good people. Key people and partners were as follows:

- FMS Inc.—The amount of $18,000 turned into a lot more when FMS decided to become a Hot Mommas® Project sponsor. They gave us additional hours of software development as part of that sponsorship.
- Students—I offered students—really, really smart students—the educational opportunity of a lifetime: work in tandem with me, work in tandem with FMS, really *learn* how a venture runs versus just fetching coffee. Sure, it took a lot more time than just hiring someone who was trained. But I was walking the talk of helping the next generation through role modeling. That was important to me.
- The George Washington University School of Business—The Development and Communications offices at GWSB threw their hats into the ring 100 percent. In my insider's blog, I've talked about research around blueprint companies that grew to over a billion dollars in revenue. Having a *key* partner was one of the success factors. We have that in the George Washington University School of Business. I had been teaching there for six years. There was a relationship. There was trust. It was—and is—a very good thing.

While the Hot Mommas® Project has existed since 2002, I kicked it into high gear over a period of six months in 2008, working part-time. In doing so, I learned an important lesson, the lesson of "superlatives." It's sort of like when you get the Presidential Physical Fitness Test gold patch for doing embarrassing activities in front of your classmates. If you only have a little bit of time (a.k.a. me—married, mom of two, on-and-off caregiver to various older folks in my life . . . yada, yada), go for the gold. I said, "Hey, I think I can build the world's largest free case library in two or three days a week." I did it and now I can hang my hat on this accomplishment, even when I'm changing diapers.

Kathy Korman Frey

KEY SUCCESS FACTORS: Good Idea, Action-Orientation, Money (And The Baggage That Goes With It), "Teeth" (Credibility), Courage, Visibility, People, Partners, The Law Of Superlatives, and a High Pain Threshold, Which is Known More Diplomatically as Tenacity

RECOMMENDED BOOKS: *The Girls' Guide to Building a Million-Dollar Business* by Susan Wilson Solovic, *The Art of the Start* by Guy Kawasaki, *The Four Hour Work Week* by Tim Ferriss, *Total Leadership* by Stuart Friedman, The Twilight Series (I had to entertain myself somehow through all of this.)

WEB SITE: www.HotMommasProject.org

EDITOR'S NOTES: Kathy Korman Frey lives in Washington DC with her husband, Josh; kids, Maxwell and Lilah; dog, Foxy; and Blackberry, Fiona. At the time of this story, Kathy is in the middle of fundraising in a horrid economy for the next generation of the Hot Mommas® Project case wizard, a Washington Post Magazine article is pending, and Hot Mommas from as far as Egypt are trekking to the first annual Hot Mommas Project awards ceremony. In her ongoing fight to balance, Kathy has started a love-hate relationship with a personal trainer to try to prioritize health over her tendency to succumb to general chaos. She is currently working on a book, *How to Be a Hot Momma*.

CHAPTER SIX

IT'S ALL ABOUT THE SERVICE

> *Express your admiration for the traits, possessions or accomplishments of your customer. Little things mean a lot.*
> —*Brian Tracy*

People rarely succeed unless they have fun in what they are doing.

—Dale Carnegie

WE DID IT OUR WAY

Even as children, my business partner, Aaron D. Dowen, and I were always doing things differently. On one occasion, we were building a tree fort and it started to become dark. Typical eleven-year-olds would have given up and gone home—not Aaron and me. We trekked back to my father's shed, pulled out a large generator and several heavy-duty lights, and dragged it all the length of a football field back to our location. We went to work with our construction site fully illuminated.

Aaron and I also had a special handshake when we said "Toyota," referring to the Toyota vans we thought looked humorous at the time. And once, we actually built an airplane. Whether it was flyable or not was beside the point. It was this thought process and ability to do what others might have thought was impossible that led us to where we are today. Aaron and I always had the mentality to live life to the fullest. Looking back at our friendship and business history, I can't help but smile.

Aaron and I always knew the key to any successful venture was dedication and innovation. In 1999, when we were eleven years old, Aaron was always working on computers and had taught himself several computer-programming languages. Our first Web site, where Aaron implemented the latest Web features, included a database of airplane pictures. With this conceptual knowledge of Web site development, we decided to sell a site. Our first customer was in the construction industry. Going into that first sales meeting with the directors of the company was one of the most difficult challenges we had ever faced. Upon our arrival at the meeting room, there was a wave of laughter at two boys in suits lugging in a rented projector, diagrams, and prospectus. However, Aaron and I were one step ahead of these directors. We had already put together a Web site, which meant they could see exactly what we were selling them. In addition, we had implemented features that were new to the Internet technology world, such as Flash and certain HTML functions. I always considered myself the "salesperson" of the partnership, so I delivered the presentation. After one hour of speaking, I opened the floor to questions. There was silence. The first person who spoke was the president of the company, who loved the design. They were extremely impressed with our hard work.

Our beginning overhead was very low since our labor, at age eleven, was practically valueless in monetary terms. With money saved up from cutting lawns, we were able to purchase the necessary Web site development software. Naming the company was another task. We wanted something that directly described our work philosophy toward customers, which was to give them the best services and products. And so, Alps Technology was founded.

Once we had secured our first deal, we were able to retain some of our earnings, invest in commodities, and reinvest in the company. Our first customer was so enthusiastic he spoke with other industry leaders about our company. Growing from two to twelve employees in two years, Alps was headed in the right direction. In 2001, our newly founded board of directors decided to invest in purchasing and maintaining our own database systems. This investment allowed us to maintain Web sites for a broader customer base—automotive dealerships, large construction firms, and industrial companies.

In 2002, we noticed a decrease in the demand for Web site development. Within six months, our associates strategically developed a new service—providing hardware, software, and consulting for companies. This service is in high demand by companies that are not large enough to have an on-site technological division. In addition, Aaron and I began a joint venture, the Alps Lawn Company, in the landscape and horticultural service industry. With a completely different client base, Aaron and I faced new challenges in a struggling Michigan economy. With innovation and strategic marketing programs, we were able to target specific customers. Within the residential sector of the market, Alps targets executive estates and larger residential developments. Direct customer reference plays a large role in the expansion of this territory. In the commercial sector, Alps targets larger office complexes, municipal organizations, and educational facilities. This sector relies on several hundred bids per year, as well as on finding the right vendor-customer combination. The marketing strategies of both Alps companies are very similar, with customer satisfaction as our number one priority.

The Alps Lawn Company successfully acquired the grounds maintenance contract for Notre Dame Preparatory School, my alma mater, six months after I graduated. The campus is eighty-eight-plus acres containing two baseball fields and over one thousand trees and shrubs, as well as an eight-plus acre parking lot, for which we provide snow-removal services in the winter.

The key to our success with this company was that Aaron and I learned every aspect of landscape management. During our first year in business, we cut the grass, read landscape literature, and learned from other professionals in the industry. The Alps Lawn Company used the latest technology. One of my hobbies is flying: I first soloed at fifteen years of age. Aaron and I have integrated my flight abilities and aerial photography to promote landscaping projects by giving clients a bird's-eye view of their properties. We were chosen by many clients just because of this unique service. In addition, Alps Technology has developed a computer-aided design (CAD) landscape software to visually show our clients what their landscape project will look like—not just show them blueprints on a sheet of paper.

In 2008, Alps took another direction. The Alps Holding Group was founded to manage the assets of both Alps Technology and the Alps Lawn Company while providing investment services and consulting. Shortly thereafter, the board of directors decided it was time to merge the three companies into one enterprise—Alps International. In addition, we integrated a new customer care center in Portland, Oregon.

Another very important aspect of business is ethical decisions and giving back to the community. For one three-day weekend each summer, all of the Michigan-based employees from Alps International work at the United Urban Foundation, a local organization that constructs homes for the less fortunate. Over this weekend, we learn more about the people we work with every day and grow as a team in order to produce the final outcome—the home. In addition to our volunteer time of approximately fifty hours, the Alps Lawn Company contributes approximately $25,000 in landscaping supplies/material to help beautify the homes. Our employees feel great about contributing the final touch and are rewarded when they see the smiles on the faces of the family members who will live in the new home. It is also rewarding for me to watch our employees grow as citizens of the community.

We also donate select landscape management services to Notre Dame Preparatory each year. Notre Dame Preparatory provided the foundation for my successful business career, so I am more than happy to donate.

The most valuable advice I could give to any aspiring entrepreneur is to really enjoy what field you are pursuing. In order for any successful organization to grow, the founders must be in it for the right reasons. When I speak at educational institutions, the students typically ask me about salaries and pay for our employees. This is not why Aaron and I have joined the industries in which we innovate. We have always had a passion for success, innovation, and technological integration. We enjoy working each day with the organizations to which we belong. In 2008, we received the prestigious Ernst & Young Entrepreneur of the Year award for our business efforts and achievements. This is not only substantial motivation to pursue advancement within our industries, but is a real compliment to us for our efforts.

What makes our story unique is that we established not one but two companies in two completely different industries—Internet technology / software development and the horticultural service industry. Over the course of founding these businesses, we have faced many obstacles and barriers, including establishing professional relationships with corporate clients and getting them to do business with a younger person. We really had to take everything a step farther when approaching a deal, from enhancing the level of professionalism to keeping a solid reference list. Many people we considered role models have told us to sell the businesses, as running them would be too much with school. Aaron and I turned their comments into motivation. Every day we would think about what they said and used it for fuel to continue—and I am graduating from the University of Michigan one and a half years early.

Being an entrepreneur is not a nine-to-five job; it requires real dedication, passion, ambition, and motivation. There are still times I work seven days a week, but I enjoy each minute of it. Business and entrepreneurs are the future. My advice is not to listen to people who tell you it is impossible to begin and run a business. In addition to a strong work ethic, I recommend pursuing a career that interests you. You have to have a passion for what you do. I know that's been said a million times, but it really is true if you want to be successful.

We have always contributed our success to our foundation principles:

- Customer Retention
- Recognizing Potential Investments and Innovating Industry Standards
- Establishing Strong Cliental Base
- Maintaining Superior Level of Professionalism
- Delivering Products/Services = Results
- Leaders + Motivation = Success
- Time Management Proficiency

Joseph A. Pascaretta   *Aaron D. Dowen*

KEY SUCCESS FACTORS: Customer Service, Determination, Passion

RECOMMENDED BOOKS: *See You at the Top* by Zig Ziglar

WEB SITE: www.alpstechnology.com, www.alpslawn.com

EDITOR'S NOTES: Mr. Pascaretta is the Chairman and Chief Executive Officer of Alps International. He currently lives in Rochester, Michigan, and plans to attend the University of Michigan MBA program. Mr. Dowen is the President and Chief Technology Officer of Alps International and resides in Niceville, Florida, with his spouse and two dogs.

Success is the sum of small efforts, repeated day in and day out.

—Robert Collier

A CUT ABOVE THE OTHERS

"You can go to the Fun House after you finish mowing the yard," my mom declared. Why was it that none of the other kids in my neighborhood (or my ninth-grade class, for that matter) had to be their mother's personal landscaper? By the age of fifteen, I had mastered knowledge of the lawn mower, weed eater, edger, fertilizer spreader, leaf blower, hedge trimmer, and just about any other tool that served a purpose in the yard. Additionally, I had a tough boss! I couldn't just mow the yard; our yard had to be meticulously manicured. The lines had to be diagonally zigzagged, so the final result was to have perfect squares throughout the regularly fertilized zoysia grass. The edges of the lawn were not to meet the concrete of the sidewalk on either side. The mulch around the Japanese maple was to have a slight slope up to the trunk of the tree in a four-foot-diametric circle, and the pruning of the gold euonymus shrubs was a science in itself. Granted, I had the help of my father at times; but my older sister's house chores didn't compare to the laborious work I was forced to perform. Neighbors never failed to comment on the wonderful upkeep of our yard. And my mom never failed to recognize my hard work by patting me on the back with the compliments we received. But I wanted more than a pat on the back and my lame weekly allowance.

When I looked down the street at the shabby yards in our neighborhood, I saw an opportunity—an opportunity to use the equipment my parents had invested in to gain a profit for myself. Our parents had given my sister a car on her sixteenth birthday, but it wasn't the nicest, to say the least. They set a limit on how much money they would contribute to our first cars, and they didn't consider inflation when determining the amount. And they would purchase my car *four years* after hers! So I was fully aware of the fact that unless I wanted to take my first date out in a boat on wheels, I needed to start saving money. Because the neighbors had seen me sweating the summer away in our yard, they already knew I had the attention to detail required to maintain good curb appeal. So earning business was easy. After going door-to-door, I had enough customers to keep me busy every day of the week; and at fifteen bucks a pop, I was banking! Of course, nobody else's standards were as high as my mother's, so caring for their yards didn't take half the time or effort as caring for our own yard, giving me time to complete multiple yards a day, if necessary. Pushing the mower through the neighborhood led to the purchase of the black Bronco I had my eye on for months leading up to my December birthday.

Like many of my friends, I got a job at Cafe Ole during high school. While I was raised to respect authority, I quickly learned I didn't like working for someone else. Believe it or not, there are politics even in the restaurant industry, as became apparent to me when *my* requested schedule wasn't honored, while *John* never worked a day he requested off. When spring returned, I was anxious to get behind my mower again. That next summer, I made my first investment in what would soon become a full-time business. Now more than ten years later, I have an inventory of lawn equipment in excess of $20,000 aside from the work trucks I maintain.

The driving motivation has always been keeping happy customers and seeing the results of my work. It provides immediate gratification. Looking back over the last decade, I have many more positive memories than negative. There have been challenges along the way, though. Lawn maintenance is seasonal for the most part. The big challenge was to keep busy throughout the off-season, especially after I hired help who relied on the income the spring and summer months provided. My solution was to expand the services Stewart Lawn and Landscape provided. Today we offer a multitude of services—full-service lawn maintenance, tree trimming, fertilization, leaf-and-tree removal, snow-and-ice removal, Christmas light installation, fencing installation and repair, and more. My staff of seven continues to stay busy year-round. Another challenge I've faced over the years has been maintaining a hardworking staff. Turnover is extremely high in this industry. For this reason, when I'm looking to staff an open position, I'm thorough in explaining my employment expectations, and I follow up by checking professional references to confirm past employment behavior. Past behavior provides great insight as to what to expect for future behavior.

The biggest success I've had over the years has been the continual expansion of our customer base. Hard work, word of mouth, and a little bit of marketing have served my business quite well. While I don't maintain a firm business plan, my vision for the future of this company is the expansion of what's already in place. My personal ethics and hardworking personality motivate those who work alongside me. As long as the service we provide continues to exceed the expectations of our customers, our ongoing success is inevitable.

Aside from the immediate gratification of seeing the results from the work, I find gratification in knowing I can provide work for another person. My crew is like family, and we all work together very well. The burden of always having work for them has been stressful at times, but providing financially for those who put forth such great effort year-round is a wonderful feeling.

Jesse Stewart
Contributed by Jocelyn Markert

KEY SUCCESS FACTORS: Customer Service, Perseverance, Work Ethic, Valuing People

RECOMMENDED BOOKS: *Stronger than Steel* by R. C. Sproul

EDITOR'S NOTES: Jesse Stewart offers the following advice to entrepreneurs: You don't have to invent something to be an entrepreneur. You just need to do something better than anyone else.

You keep customers by delivering on your promises, fulfilling your commitments, and continually investing in the quality of your relationships.
—Brian Tracy

A BALANCED LIFE

"Go ahead and do it . . . as long as it doesn't cost me any money!" These were the words of conditional support offered by my husband when I shared my entrepreneurial plans to open a massage therapy practice of my own. His "encouragement" neither surprised nor disappointed me, as I have been married to this fiscally conservative man for twenty years and quite expected this point of view.

In fact, I was used to it, having been raised in a middle-class family with a wonderful father who took great care of his wife and three children through years of hard work and little fun. He served in the U.S. Navy for twenty-one years and then worked for a large corporation until he retired at age fifty-five. His life example taught me not to take big risks. He was extra cautious about financial matters. He avoided confrontation and didn't like anyone to rock the boat. My dad's attitude about work was to "get a job with a good retirement plan." His philosophy shaped my expectations for my own career as I graduated from college and found a job with the same large corporation, with a promise of a moderate salary and a good retirement plan. There, I was relegated to a cubicle-style work space, performing unfulfilling tasks for a company that didn't know me from the other ten thousand employees, all of whom were insignificant and easily replaced as needed. My dad often lamented about his daily grind with a dramatic and tired sigh: "What a life!" We all knew he didn't really enjoy his job, but he faithfully worked every day to support his family. This is a common theme for many people with a weekly schedule that allows for little more than work, eat, sleep, and get up and do it all over again. Well, that job didn't suit me very well. The clock at the office seemed to run slower and slower, and I tried to imagine myself elsewhere doing meaningful work. My rescue appeared in the form of an engagement ring and the promise of a better life.

Fast-forward a few years, and I am a married mother of two. Like most traditional wives and mothers, my family is my primary "job." Any ideas I had for starting my own business were quickly sent to the back burner. They simmered there for years as I took excellent care of my family first. My father's cautionary words against high risk and low security were deeply rooted. My husband's fiscal philosophy to save a lot and spend a little influenced me greatly to wait a little longer before pursuing self-employment.

I have worked as a massage therapist for the past eight years and in a successful private practice of my own for the past two and a half years. This entrepreneurial venture evolved slowly after working in a salon and spa for several years. I developed my skills as a therapist, built a loyal client base, and learned a lot about business ownership and management as I performed many supervisory responsibilities for this operation. This experience gave me the knowledge and skills to run my own business and the confidence to do it in a way that was better for me. I basically outgrew my situation as an employee and desired the independence of setting up a massage practice with my personal brand of customer service, a more flexible work schedule, and creative control as a business owner.

To the money-driven, super-ambitious, career-minded individual, my experience may seem unimpressive. However, my success as an entrepreneur is best measured by my success as a wife and mother. I schedule all my work appointments with consideration for my family's plans, school events, church obligations, volunteer committees, exercise time, and lunch dates with my friends—an arrangement that gives me great balance and variety in every workday. I am healthier and happier than I have ever been. I also earn more income than I ever did as an employee. My biggest challenge in owning this business is learning to say no. For the sake of my own self-care, time management, and quality attention to my important relationships with family and friends, I am restricted in the amount of work I can do. My practice is full, with high retention of loyal clients who appreciate my expertise. My work is fulfilling in the knowledge that what I do matters and makes a difference to others. My personal characteristics of being organized, hard-working, practical, fair, and honest helped me to develop and maintain a profitable business. Being conscientious, nurturing, generous, spiritual, and a good listener makes me a great massage therapist, someone whom my clients trust with their care and well-being.

A small picture frame in my office reveals a quotation by Maya Angelou that perfectly expresses how I feel about my life: "People will forget what you said; people will forget what you did; but people will never forget how you made them feel." This is the secret of my success as an entrepreneur—I feel affirmed and important. I feel my life matters to others. I feel others care about me. This is what I try to share with my clients, with my family, with my friends, and in my life. Entrepreneurship gives me the freedom to have the balanced life I want and to have it on my own terms.

C. C. Crane
Contributed by Heather Arena

KEY SUCCESS FACTORS: Outstanding Product, Excellent Service, Being Generous

RECOMMENDED BOOKS: *Massage Therapy: Career Guide for Hands-On Success* by Steve Capellini

EDITOR'S NOTES: C. C. Crane lives with her husband, Patrick; daughter, Kelly; and son, Davis, in Stillwater, Oklahoma. Patrick has been employed locally for over fifteen years. Kelly is a student at the University of Oklahoma, and Davis attends Stillwater High School.

C. C. is extremely consistent in offering a great massage that is therapeutic, professional, and customized for each client's needs. She is generous with her time, typically working longer than the massage session is scheduled. She is also generous with the extras, which add comfort, such as using a heated massage pad and providing hot stones for the back, a hot towel for the neck, bottled water, and extra blankets when needed. And finally, she is generous with her attention, allowing plenty of time during each appointment for clients to discuss recent ailments and changes in their body's wellness. She identifies problem areas that are noticed during the session and then shares resources for the client's health and well-being, such as improving diet, posture, exercise, and stretching. C. C. likes knowing her clients are getting an incredible value for their money. In fact, it's not uncommon to have clients say, "That was the best massage I've ever had!"

Learn to listen. Opportunity could be knocking at your door very softly.

—Anonymous

BREAKING THE BARRIERS

I had to take several steps to become the woman I am today. I always strived to do my absolute best and to be the best. I graduated as valedictorian of my high school class and majored in mathematics at the University of Oklahoma from 1966 to 1968. Cosmetology, however, was my real interest—I grew up in a small town in the sixties when hair was magnificent! I promised my mother if she allowed me to attend cosmetology school, I would finish college and receive my degree at a later point in time. She agreed, and I graduated from beauty college in December of 1968. Afterward, I attended the University of Tulsa from 1969 to 1978, trying to fulfill my end of the deal, but eventually dropped out. In 1998, I returned to the University of Tulsa and graduated with a Bachelor's Degree in Finance in December of 2008.

My first job as a hairstylist was at Miss Jackson's salon from 1970 to 1980. I liked working for Miss Jackson's but became frustrated with the salon's lack of continuing education, the inability to create Sassoon-style cuts, the fact the salon was not open on evenings, and the salon's failure to provide cuts for male clients. I decided there had to be a better way.

I was the single mother of two small boys and had a mortgage; but in 1980, I was able to take out a SBA loan to open my very first salon. A client informed me of a shopping center she was opening on Brookside, and after deciding it was a great location, I opened the doors to my first location in Tulsa, Oklahoma. I opened the salon with only three hairdressers, three manicurists, and a front desk employee. I created a business plan; but as the company grew, I realized my first effort had been fairly weak. And as I added locations, my business plan became, and has remained, highly detailed. I created a salon culture I believe in, including in-salon education, wellness, leadership, and excellence. I have faced several challenges, such as never having enough money or enough time; but I was very skilled at my craft, and having a large clientele helped to overcome the deficits.

My current salon locations offer updated, trendy hairstyles and colors to a wide variety of clients, including men. The atmosphere is friendly, both for my clients and for my employees. I worked behind the chair until 1998, when I decided to work on the business instead of in it. In 2002, both my sons joined the company to help with expansion and marketing. At that time, we had fifty employees. We now have 145. Continuing with our success, in 2008, the Ihloff Salon was featured in *Elle* magazine as the best salon in Oklahoma!

The best thing about being an entrepreneur is having the independence to create the culture in which you believe. I moved my original salon from a shopping center on Brookside to an upscale shopping area in Utica Square and expanded it into a full-service salon and day spa. Earlier that year, I opened my second location on Eighty-third Street and Memorial Drive in South Tulsa. Both locations house a salon and day spa, operate at full employee capacity, and focus on creating an experience for each guest through guest care and Aveda products. In March of 2007, I opened my third salon location in Kansas City, Kansas; and shortly after, in March of 2009, my fourth salon location opened in Norman, Oklahoma. We have a Web site that contains information on services for all four locations, as well as a business center in Tulsa that focuses on guest care through the scheduling of appointments. Communication is difficult with growth, yet it is critical to the success of any company, as are values and having a shared vision.

Cosmetology is a very disparate industry, and cosmetology schools do not effectively train for professionalism or focus on the importance of continuing education once a license has been achieved. Because I believe continuing education is very important, stylists at all four locations complete an assistant training program lasting between nine months to a year before becoming a stylist in the salon. The program requires future stylists to shadow master stylists and learn from them; it also requires trainees to complete forty-eight educational classes taught by Aveda instructors and salon master stylists. After completion of this program, stylists can start on the floor at the salon location of their choice as a protégé, or entry-level stylist. They receive promotions by accomplishing in-salon goals and work their way through eight stylist levels to progress to the advanced master level, where a service provider has the flexibility to set their own schedule and price level.

I believe learning should never stop; entrepreneurs and service providers should read business books and anything that motivates them to succeed. The community recognizes me for being a true environmental leader, entrepreneur, and businesswoman, who sets new standards for salons across the state. Our company is committed to the community, and we are always engaged in some form of community involvement. We hold major community events in the spring and the fall. In the spring, we do an event around sustainability and Earth Month called Refresh Tulsa, usually benefiting Up with Trees of Tulsa. In the fall, we do a hair show event, which benefits Resonance, a center for women. This past year, we raised around $50,000 to benefit the women, volunteers, and staff of Resonance. We also participate in a quarterly United Way campaign for employees in all locations, as well as allow our staff to wear jeans on Fridays for a $5 donation to Sustainable Tulsa.

I have learned a lot from my journey as an entrepreneur. There have been plenty of challenges and struggles, but I wouldn't change a thing. There have never been any failures or regrets; *failure* is not a word with which I am comfortable. I believe in living in the moment, and when there are challenges, adjusting and learning from them. There are drawbacks to being an entrepreneur, such as not having a set schedule and working more hours throughout the week than expected; however, the rewards far outweigh the drawbacks. We as a company and as a team succeed each time a team member reaches a goal, pleases a guest, or improves their lives; and we celebrate these successes each day. Success to me is growing a healthy team and serving happy guests in an atmosphere of teamwork, excellence, wellness, and learning. I also want to give back to an industry that has given me a full and happy life—and of course, profitability, so we can keep the doors open!

If I could offer advice to anyone wanting to be an entrepreneur, I would suggest researching the industry, such as its costs and opportunities for profitability, barriers to entry, and time commitment. The biggest strength and most important aspect of my company is the heart of our organization, which is a very strong and wonderful team. Each has a servant's heart and a warrior's spirit, and all are supported by strategic planning, careful execution, and committed management.

Marilyn Ihloff
Contributed by Amber Baldwin

KEY SUCCESS FACTORS: Customer Service, Having the Right Team, Work Ethic

WEB SITE: *www.ihloffspa.com*

EDITOR'S NOTES: Marilyn Ihloff is the owner of Ihloff Salon and Day Spa in Tulsa. She has been the sole owner of Ihloff Salon and Day Spa for over twenty-eight years and operates four locations in Kansas City, Norman, and Tulsa, Oklahoma. Marilyn currently lives in midtown Tulsa and recently became a proud grandmother to a granddaughter and a grandson. She has a boxer dog named Edward and loves to take him to the Tulsa Bark Park for fun on the weekends.

Marilyn is in the process of opening Oklahoma's first Aveda Institute, a high—quality beauty school providing Aveda education with a certification. The school should open in downtown Tulsa within the next few years. A pioneer in sustainability and environmental leadership, Marilyn has recently hired a new cleaning company for both Tulsa locations, Total Clean Up, which is an environmentally friendly, green-cleaning company, using natural, safe products to clean the salon every night.

Knowledge comes, but wisdom lingers.
—Alfred Lord Tennyson

BUILDING A REPUTATION OF EXCELLENCE

The skyline in the growing northwest quadrant of San Antonio, Texas, has changed over the past twenty years from the rolling quiet hill country of brush and oak trees to a busy, productive city. Part of that skyline of neatly built office buildings was created by MDM Development. My wife, Katherine, and I have been constructing buildings and commercial properties in San Antonio for more than twenty years. We purchase properties in distress, using an evaluation system to determine why the property struggled to be profitable, and upgrade them. We also renovate large commercial properties and have built several office buildings and complexes.

I began my career in the commercial lending business after graduating from the University of Texas in Arlington in 1974 with a degree in Finance. In my job as a commercial lender, I evaluated properties for financing, down to the minute details. The financing company monitored the progress of large properties; but as I watched their progress, I realized many projects were not being monitored appropriately. Many clients did not watch the financial details of their commercial project carefully. Maybe they did not oversee their contractors, or they might not supervise the project in such a way as to guide decision making. Many times, poor decisions were made because of no oversight. Thus, I decided I could be successful in building a commercial project if I were just careful with all the details. I also felt I had a talent for supervising.

Because of limited capital, my first project had to be profitable. Through my job at the bank, I was very aware of the need for commercial warehousing in San Antonio. I felt confident if I could build a commercial warehouse in the right location in the growing northwest part of San Antonio, I could keep it leased and profitable. I spent every free moment scouring the town, looking for the right property in the right location with easy access to the main highways. Fortunately, I found a location that fit my needs.

Once I found the location for this commercial warehouse, I had to quit my job and get financing. I knew this decision was right and was able to convince a lender to provide the financing. I spent a great deal of time on the details of this project and chose the most capable of contractors. I wanted to work with people of professional integrity, not just those who offered the lesser bid. It was more important to do a job of excellence. As a result, I have developed a reputation among the San Antonio building industry, and contractors and subcontractors are eager to work for me.

My first project went smoothly. When it was almost complete and ready for leasing, a Mexican national investor group offered me a substantial cash price for the project. Their offer was a nice surprise, and the cash helped give me the capital for the next project.

My next project was also important. I spotted a building, noticed there were not many cars in the parking lot, and speculated about why the building was struggling. After purchasing the building, I developed a team including an architect and a space planner to evaluate the building. They came up with a different design and the architecture was adjusted. The building took off. It was fully occupied and became very profitable. Once again, a buyer offered us a substantial amount for the building, helping capitalize the company even more and making it possible for us to move to more aggressive projects.

I had to overcome the cost overruns that are part of every building project. They are a fact of the industry. Because of cost overruns, I have to micromanage each project—one poor decision can cost its profitability.

Personnel issues can also be difficult. One situation involved an employee. He became a vital part of the company and even supervised his own projects. He departed, leaving a major hole in the company. The projects he had been working on were left in the lurch. I had to jump in and work constantly to keep the company afloat.

I give back to the community through varied activities. I am very active in a business organization named the National Association of Industrial and Office Properties. I support local seminars on various topics by providing papers to support data. These exchanges are helpful to me, as well as contributing to the real estate professional community. This organization supports young entrepreneurs from local colleges and universities who have an interest in real estate development. I hope to mentor these young people and help them live the life I have enjoyed as an entrepreneur.

Reuben Trevino
Contributed by Jackie Legg Sartin

KEY SUCCESS FACTORS: Customer Support, Courage, Expertise, Communication, Responsiveness

EDITOR'S NOTES: Reuben and Katherine Trevino own and operate MDM Development in San Antonio, Texas, and provide extraordinary customer support.

CHAPTER SEVEN

OVERCOMING THE UNEXPECTED

In the middle of difficulty lies opportunity.
— *Albert Einstein*

Always bear in mind that your own resolution to succeed is more important than any other one thing.
                                —*Abraham Lincoln*

ENTREPRENEUR4LIFE

Since the age of seven, I have been an entrepreneur. I started by collecting cans, delivering newspapers, and doing numerous odd jobs on the inner city streets of Chicago, Illinois. My childhood dream was to become a real estate investor and relocate my mother and my sister away from our crime-infested neighborhood. My father died of esophageal cancer when I was three years old, leaving my mother to raise us alone in a one-room tenement, with rats as large as my size 12 shoes and cockroaches that could fly. Abuse, violence, and drug use were constant throughout my household and surroundings. At school and in my neighborhood, I was an outcast. I was never considered good enough and I was constantly picked on and bullied. Entrepreneurship became my outlet and my first love, and it kept me from getting involved in selling drugs or joining one of Chicago's notorious street gangs. Entrepreneurship and my imagination helped me maintain a good attitude throughout my adolescence.

In spring of 1991, when I was fourteen, my mother, my sister, and I relocated to Tulsa, Oklahoma, to live with my mother's sister. Initially, I had mixed feelings because it was difficult to go from a metropolis that operated 24/7 to a place where most of the grocery stores closed at 9:00 p.m. and the streets were quiet as a mouse. After a few weeks in Tulsa, I started doing what I enjoyed and knew best, entrepreneurship. I began by mowing yards. I came from a place where the only grass grew in the concrete cracks. After seeing all the trees and yards in Tulsa, I immediately capitalized on an opportunity to mow yards and make money. I applied and was hired by a community-summer-jobs-for-youth organization to do landscaping throughout the summer of 1991.

While browsing through the business opportunities section in the *Tulsa World*, I spotted an advertisement that mentioned gumball vending machines for sale. From my days on the streets of Chicago, I had wanted to become involved in the vending business. I called the number in the advertisement and a salesman from Oklahoma City drove to Tulsa to do a demonstration. After reviewing the product, I was immediately sold and purchased one machine. I took advantage of their free placement service and located the machine inside a barbecue restaurant on the other side of town. It brought in between $100 and $200 a week. I was on top of the world!

From the monies earned in vending, I started purchasing M&M's and candy bars in large amounts from the local Sam's Club and other food wholesalers and sold them door-to-door. I really enjoyed the freedom of setting my own hours and not asking anyone for cash. I also sold candy to my classmates in middle school and to local businesses. I soon realized the importance of leverage. Leverage is your greatest friend if you know how to use it. It has made billionaires—and paupers. A classmate told me about this guy named Glenn. He hired youth between the ages of fourteen and sixteen to sell candy bars for him. I thought about the benefits of no longer putting up money to purchase the candy, the wide range of areas I could sell them, and the increased profit I could make selling candy bars for Glenn. I immediately joined the sales team. As I look back on these experiences, I almost come to tears thinking about the independence and freedom I had to earn a living for myself at an early age. My sales endeavor with Glenn continued through my ninth-grade year in high school.

At the age of sixteen, I became very interested in the entertainment business and had dreams of becoming a musician. I called various record labels in New York, California, and Chicago. I ran up my mother's long distance bill trying to get signed to a record deal. When I was fifteen, I invested in studio time with Tulsa-famed musician/producer and studio engineer Lonnie Liggett and created a music demo. I was dead set on becoming a superstar in the entertainment industry. It was during my tenth-grade year, one spring day in 1994, when I opened this big package from a record label in Fairfield, California. I discovered numerous cassettes, posters, T-shirts, and about fifty blank fill-out forms. They didn't want to sign me to a record deal. Because of my persistence, they recruited me as a record promoter. I immediately went to my high school and signed up my classmates to receive free promotional products from this record company. I was paid $1 for each name and address I submitted. After a while, I started to become noticed by my peers, and they wanted to hang out with me. Throughout school, I had been an outcast, and now I felt I was getting my due.

During the summer break, I travelled to Chicago to visit friends. When I came back to Tulsa, I brought clothing to sell. The styles of clothing they had in Chicago were not available in Tulsa, so I capitalized off the Style Arbitrage. Those were the good ole days! At various times during my teen years (in addition to selling candy bars for Glenn), I had a paper route for the now-defunct *Tulsa Sentinel* and jobs at Simple Simon's Pizza and Braum's ice cream store. I held these jobs while I attended Memorial High School. I truly loved what I was doing. In hindsight, I'm glad I was exposed to these experiences because they prepared me for what was to come.

During my tenth-grade year, I was fed up with being a loner and not being totally accepted by my peers. The majority of people in my neighborhood were in the streets doing whatever it took to get by—which involved drugs, gangs, and violence. I thought I would do the same. It seemed simple because I had grown up around it all my life. I was kicked out of my first high school for breaking the law. I was in and out of juvenile lockup facilities. I didn't care about anything. I went to another high school, but dropped out before I turned seventeen. I thought school was for fools. Besides, I thought I was going to earn a lot of money being a big-time hip-hop performer and owning real estate. Throughout these misguided times, I always had a legitimate job. I was convinced selling drugs was worse than having a minimum-wage job. Drug addicts want to get high not only from nine to five; they want to get high twenty-four hours a day. That means sellers have to be awake and on the street all the time.

In 1997, at the age of nineteen, after coming home from a friend's house, I got into a fight with my mother's boyfriend. I ended up lying facedown in feces and urine in the middle of the living room floor for twelve hours, turning my head from side to side, struggling to breathe, and begging for help. My sister found me the next day and called the ambulance. I didn't know what happened but I couldn't move my arms or legs. I woke up in the hospital with the doctor telling me I had a severely broken neck, a C4 complete spinal cord injury, and I would be paralyzed (a quadriplegic) for the rest of my life.

For the first couple of years, I had issues. I had a very hard time dealing with my new life and my feelings of anger, suicide, abandonment, and depression. The moment of change came when I decided (due to my growing faith in God and encouragement from friends) to achieve a GED. I later enrolled in college, embarked on a public-speaking career, and completed physical rehabilitation so I might have the possibility of walking again. Most importantly, I forgave my mother and her boyfriend.

I returned to my entrepreneurial endeavors selling nursing uniforms, perfume, and clothing. The employees of the nursing home and my classmates in college were my loyal customers. In 2002, I received an Associates of Science Degree from Tulsa Community College; and in 2005, I received a Bachelor's Degree in Business Administration with a major in Marketing from Oklahoma State University, where my friend and mentor, T. Boone Pickens, gave the commencement speech. Also, because of my passion and interest in trading and investing, I passed the Series 3 commodities futures exam in May of 2006. The nursing home where I have been living for the past ten years was been very supportive of my endeavors. They arranged for me to have a private room in addition to sending me on a vacation to Las Vegas and giving me a desktop computer as a gift for my educational accomplishments. In 2003, I received assistance from friend and business maven T. Boone Pickens in the form of a sponsorship to consult with the former doctors of Christopher Reeve at the Barnes-Jewish Hospital / Washington School of Medicine in St. Louis, Missouri, along with the International Center for Spinal Cord Injury at the Kennedy Krieger Institute in Baltimore, Maryland. I was also fortunate to meet and befriend a Guinness World Record holder for the first quadriplegic in the world who ever walked again, Patrick Rummerfield. He is a leading advocate for spinal cord injury research and development. These valuable contacts enabled me to receive specialized equipment to use in Tulsa's Center for Individuals with Physical Challenges, where individuals with similar injuries are benefiting from it also.

To date, I have regained physical improvement in the lower back / abdominal region, bowel and bladder sensation, and strength, along with minimal activity in my right leg. I believe it is my responsibility to contribute in any way I can to others. My experiences made me a stronger and wiser person. I will continue to face new challenges and meet new goals with a smile and a never-give-up entrepreneurial attitude.

Nate Waters

KEY SUCCESS FACTORS: Passion, Endurance

RECOMMENDED BOOKS: *The Luckiest Guy in the World* by T. Boone Pickens, *Fooled by Randomness: The Hidden Role of Chance in Life and in the Markets* by Nassim Nicholas Taleb

WEB SITE: *www.natewaters.com*

EDITOR'S NOTES: Nate is currently employed at the Williams Companies Inc. in Tulsa, Oklahoma, as a joint interest billing accountant in the natural gas exploration and production department. He has been creating and working on national initiatives that will decrease the high school dropout rate and teach the skills of entrepreneurship to at-risk teens to help reduce the poverty rate. Nate Waters is also involved in various nonprofit organizations like the Center for Individuals with Physical Challenges, the Bridges Foundation, the Cystic Fibrosis Foundation, H.O.P.E., and others. His public speaking is currently growing into a full-time business, and Nate is writing an autobiography.

Happiness is not a destination. It is a method of life.
—Burton Hills

HAPPINESS

Born in Fort Leonard Wood, Missouri, and raised in southern Oklahoma by two wonderful parents, Jerry and Johnnell Horn, our family was very involved in the Baptist Church, so God has always been an important part of my life. Along with two younger siblings, Jeretta and Jeffery, I was raised in a home where love, compassion, caring, and perseverance were taught and shared daily. It was also a very sheltered environment; so when I ventured into the world, I had a lot of surprises about how some people were raised and their beliefs and values.

As a sophomore in high school, a business teacher, Ms. Edith Merryman, became my mentor for my career path. She is a wonderful lady, and I will always be grateful to her. My husband of more than thirty years was also introduced to me in high school and was quickly welcomed as a member of our family. His love and support have helped me become the person I am today.

Going to college was always the plan, so I attended Southeastern Oklahoma State University in Durant, Oklahoma, where I completed a bachelor's degree. After graduation, I taught one year of special education before taking a break to give birth to my beautiful daughter, Heather Michele, and to work on my master's degree. Life was great as a happily married mother with a goal of obtaining a master's degree—*until* . . .

My dad and I were riding horses and working cattle on a beautiful spring day when the horse I was riding entered a boggy area, apparently lost control, and I fell on my head. When Dad got to me, my face was buried in mud, and I wasn't breathing. After he was sure I was breathing again, Dad said he had to do one of the hardest things he had ever done: ride out to get help, leaving me behind. My skull had been cracked from one ear around the back of my head and through the other ear. I was in intensive care and unresponsive for several days. When I became responsive, I thought I was twelve instead of twenty-two. I was temporarily paralyzed on one side and not able to talk or write. I didn't know my husband, Hi, or even my baby daughter. It took many people to help me return to life as I knew it before the accident. Although I was under the care of several doctors during the following year, I wanted to complete my master's degree. Some of the doctors felt it would be impossible; but with determination and the help from my family and a special teacher, Lois Crow at SOSU, I returned to school that summer. My dad, my mom, or my husband would drive me to Southeastern each day; and my sister, who worked at SOSU during that time, would be sure I got to class and back to my ride home. I continued to improve daily. When I was released from the doctor's care a year after my accident, I knew how old I was, who the people around me were, and who I was. There were times during that year when I very easily could have given up, when I had excruciating pain that left me unable to move my head, open my eyes in the light, or even think. My family's love and support kept me going, and I persevered and came back stronger than ever, completing my master's degree and later getting my public school counseling certification. Six years after completing my master's degree, our family was complete with the birth of a baby boy we named Jared.

I have taught and worked with people from babies to adults. One of my most rewarding accomplishments as a teacher was launching a career transitions ICE program that helps students go from school to work. It includes education about job, communication, and leadership skills and enables students to earn high school credit for on-the-job experience. As facilitator of this program, I help the students find jobs if necessary, visit them at their job sites, communicate with their employers, and collaborate with their teachers if they are having problems.

I have loved every area I have worked in and feel very fortunate to have been able to touch so many lives. My calling in life has been to help others. I am an academic entrepreneur, creatively giving myself to others. At times, it has been difficult—but laughter and love keep me going.

I believe some of the most important things in your life are happiness in what you are doing and perseverance in the areas that are important. Never give up—keep on keeping on.

Jennifer Horn Hillburn

KEY SUCCESS FACTORS: Determination, Perseverance, Positive Attitude, Family Support

RECOMMENDED BOOKS: *Better Than Good: Creating a Life You Can't Wait to Live* by Zig Ziglar, *Don't Sweat the Small Stuff at Work: Simple Ways to Minimize Stress and Conflict While Bringing Out the Best in Yourself and Others* by Richard Carlson, PhD, the poem *Footprints,* author unknown

EDITOR'S NOTE: Jennifer has recently retired but is continuing to work with high school students in job careers and is on the Board of Equestrian Therapy for children and adults. Jennifer lives with her husband, Hi, in Colbert, Oklahoma and has a son, Jared; a daughter, Heather; a son-in-law, David; and two wonderful grandchildren, Jack and Blair.

A desire can overcome all objections and obstacles.
　　　　　　　　　　　　　　　　　　　—Gunderson

BUILDING A LIFE

Sir Winston Churchill once said, "Success is the ability to go from one failure to another with no loss of enthusiasm." This quote has kept me focused and dedicated throughout my entrepreneurship journey. I started Jeff Davis Home Renovation and Design in January 2003 after the economic backlash from 9/11 forced me to be laid off from the technology consulting firm XOR. Deciding to hang up my fifteen-year corporate career and trade frequent-flyer miles for plywood was a big step, but now I wouldn't change anything about the decision. The years I spent in the corporate world provided me with invaluable experience that has helped me run a successful white-collar business in a blue-collar market.

But the road to entrepreneurship wasn't as smooth as I had hoped. Only five months after the launch of the business, I was in a near-fatal car crash, which left my right foot 90 percent severed. After thirteen hours of surgery, four months in a wheelchair, eight months out of work, and relearning to walk on my nerve-damaged foot, I took a long look at my situation. Without health insurance I was forced into bankruptcy and lost all the clientele I had built in the short life of my business. The outlook for Jeff's Home Renovation was bleak. But once again my "dust the dirt off and climb back on" attitude gave me the personal strength and determination to overcome all of the obstacles. I dove back into the business in January 2004, the lowest season for construction demand. Although my business faced many trials following the accident, I have been fortunate to have had only three weeks in the last five years when I didn't have a project. My greatest triumph is finally being at the top of my game. My business is now in such high demand that people are willing to wait weeks, and even months, to have their work done. The biggest change in my business, and the best, is having the option to say no. I can choose which jobs to take, as opposed to accepting every one that comes along. Previously, when my business was new, I could not be selective.

For me, success is not measured in dollars or cars, but rather, in having a happy family and job I love. I give back to the community by providing free remodeling to various nonprofit organizations throughout the Tulsa area. For example, I have remodeled bedrooms and bathrooms at St. Joseph's Monastery and at the Tulsa Glory House, a halfway house for battered women. Also, my wife and I work together in donating our time and resources to the Make-a-Wish Foundation. I am very happy and love the sense of pride I get from giving back to the community. Drive, determination, and work ethic are characteristics to which I attribute my success and happiness.

Jeff Davis
Contributed by Sydney Davis

KEY SUCCESS FACTORS: Passion, Perseverance, Work Ethic, Determination, Prioritizing

EDITOR'S NOTE: Jeff Davis lives in Tulsa with his wife and is the owner of Jeff Davis Home Renovation and Design.

Adversity is another way to measure the greatness of individuals. I never had a crisis that didn't make me stronger.
—*Lou Holtz*

LAID OFF—NO LONGER AN OPTION

When my boss walked in and said, "You are doing a great job; but the company is struggling, so we are going to have to lay you off," that was the last straw. I knew I was doing a good job. I was putting in twelve hours a day, was on the road every other week—and now I don't have a job? What's wrong with this picture? This was my third strike at being laid off, and I said "Enough."

I was at the mercy of others. I was being dictated to by higher-ups who were not in the trenches. The layoff happened at a once-cutting-edge restaurant chain that did not adapt to the eating habits of the consumers. While the bosses were still getting a salary, benefits, and a *huge* severance, I was unemployed. What did I do to deserve this? At this point, I realized by having a job, I was allowing others to control my career and financial destiny.

My assistant, who was let go before I was, contacted me to say a large company in San Francisco was seeking a new public relations firm. Between the two of us, we had thirty years of public relations expertise; and because we had no employees or overhead, we could offer our services at a more affordable price. We made contact (it took many calls, but persistence paid off), got a meeting, and presented a proposal. In a little over a month, I went from unemployed to opening Sansone & Cook Public Relations.

Sounds easy? It wasn't. But it did tell us we had something companies wanted—competitive prices and a fresh approach to PR. My industry is all about connections, so connect is exactly what we did. We spent hours cold-calling companies, talking up our services, and telling anyone who would listen—whether at a bar or coffee shop—about our new company. Within three months, we had three clients; and though we were not making a lot of money, it showed we had what it took to make money.

I believe these are great and necessary qualities for a business owner, but how do they work in a partnership? In my situation, my partnership came together by circumstances, not by evaluating and choosing an associate who complemented my skills, personality, or temperament. While trying to build a company, my partner and I were at odds on how to work within the company, and the energies spent trying to resolve our differences on a daily basis needed to be spent on growing the business. After two years, it was apparent our business styles were never going to meet, so we went our separate ways.

The end result—we both grew our companies bigger and better separately, and to this day, we continue to help champion one another's business.

After going from a partnership to sole proprietorship, I never doubted I could do it on my own. It never crossed my mind I would not be successful. Call that blind stupidity? Perhaps. But my belief is if I allowed those doubts to enter my head, there would be a greater possibility of failure. I was raised to believe whatever you do, you do to the best of your ability. I was blessed with a father who was self-employed and had the strongest work ethic I have ever known, and a mother who instilled in me confidence, a competitive edge, and a bit of feistiness.

That does not mean to ignore signals you are drowning. I have found a positive, go-for-it attitude has a greater chance of success—and it worked for me!

All of a sudden, I was cold-calling, writing proposals, pitching clients, and doing *all* the implementation of the campaign. Could I do all of it? Yes. Was it the best way to do it? No. I had to reevaluate my skills and determine what made my company profitable. It was not keeping books. It was not putting press kits together or running to the printers. I knew my strengths—meeting people, developing a campaign, and closing the deal. That does not mean I did not do other things to keep the business going, but these were the strengths that brought in the money. It became apparent to me I needed assistance in order to meet the growth goal I had set for my company.

Suddenly I went from just me to a staff of four and a larger office. Now I could do those things that made money. All was well, right? Wrong. Even though Sansone Public Relations was billing triple the amount and I was better able to focus on building the company, I felt so responsible for the employees and for maintaining a level of income to meet payroll, pay benefits and employee taxes, insurance, etc., that I fell right back where I was when I had a job—working for someone else, my staff!

Obviously, this was not what I had planned. I came up with several alternatives and narrowed it down to two. I could change how I looked at my responsibility or find another way to have people work for me where I would not have the emotions of "I need to take care of them." I offered each of them an opportunity to contract their services to me on an as-needed basis. I was also willing to assist them in finding other contractual services so it would be financially rewarding. Two opted to find other jobs and the other two said it was worth a shot.

To this day, this was one of best decisions I ever made. I continue to contract services as needed. I have the camaraderie of staff, the opportunity for creativity and brainstorming ideas, and the ability to take on more and bigger clients while maintaining my independence and being the boss.

I have now had Sansone+ (my company has evolved from public relations to an array of marketing services that include writing books, events, promotions, advertising) for twenty-two years. I am proud to say that though I have struggled at times, being an entrepreneur is what I am meant to do. I have learned to not apologize for what I charge or prostitute myself to get a client. I have had the opportunity to educate interns in assorted marketing strategies and see them go on to successful careers. I enjoy volunteering my services to specific nonprofits, bringing attention and visibility to their needs and their good work using my talent and skills. In others words, I wouldn't change a thing!

Katherine E. Sansone

KEY SUCCESS FACTORS: Confidence, Persistence, Enthusiasm for My Work and My Clients, Integrity

WEB SITE: *www.sansoneplus.com*

EDITOR'S NOTES: Katherine E. Sansone lives in Oakland, California, where she enjoys golf, running in the hills, and working out. She remains a go-getter in all aspects of her life.

A leader, once convinced that a particular course of action is the right one, must . . . be undaunted when the going gets tough.
—Ronald Reagan

CARS ARE JUST A GUY THING—NOT!

You may find it surprising that in an automotive services business, my target customers are women between the ages of twenty-five and fifty. At Trinity Restoration, we offer automotive services ranging from oil changes and detailing jobs to major collision and restoration projects. Strategically focusing on customer respect and excellent customer service within our target market has made a difference in our success.

After several tumultuous years in the telecommunications industry, I hired a business broker to help me find a Tulsa-based business that had good books, made some money, and was a business into which I could inject my marketing and sales experience to help it blossom. In 2004, my broker found Trinity Restoration, which had all the components I was looking for, with one added bonus—*cars!* I love cars! My father was a car enthusiast and mechanic, and I inherited his passion for automobiles. I took a leap, quit my telecommunications job, and bought Trinity Restoration. My passion made up for my lack of experience in automotive restoration.

My first month of ownership was very difficult because I did not earn enough to cover expenses. Fortunately, the original owner, Dennis Cockrell, stayed during the transfer of ownership, giving me time to promote my new company and rebrand Trinity's image. The next month was a little better; and by the third month, I hit a home run, almost tripling my earnings. Now I make more in one day than I made in my first entire month. What an incredible feeling and humbling experience.

In the next two years, my business continued to grow; and by 2006, I needed a much bigger shop than the original five-thousand-square-foot building. On June 30, 2007, I opened a new 25,611-square-foot state-of-the-art mechanical and restoration facility. Going from two employees in 2004 to over fifty in 2008, we are now Tulsa's best and biggest automotive mechanical and restoration company. We also hit number 1202 on the 2008 Inc. 5,000 Fastest Growing Private Companies in America list. Wow, what an honor, and a very big thank-you to our customers for making this happen!

I accomplished these incredible milestones by adding a valuable missing ingredient in the automotive repair industry—*great work combined with great customer service*. Within my industry, my competitors have not taken the time or committed to changing their current skill sets to address their customers' needs or determine their target customers. I have. Identifying my target customers as women between the ages of twenty-five and fifty, I made adjustments to my facilities by adding a children's playroom, a free coffee bar, and a clean lobby and restrooms. I have also taken the extra step to offer a Ladies' Day the first weekend of every month. On Ladies' Day, my women patrons receive discounted automotive services; and while waiting, they can enjoy free manicures and massages. In order to best reach my target customers, I have hired an all-women marketing firm, and I advertise during daytime talk shows instead of at sporting events or on sports/car networks.

Other value-added services I promote are Forever Detailing, Forever Warranty, and customer follow-ups. With every car we complete body work on, we give the owner free detailing, and we warranty our work for as long as the owner possesses the car. To show appreciation for our customers' patronage, we send thank-you letters and complete a follow-up phone call to ensure customer satisfaction.

I remind my employees not to forget what got us here—quality work and excellent service. Do the cars right, and treat the customers with respect. When a customer contacts us to repair a wrecked car, we first ask if they and their passengers are OK before discussing the car; then we explain the process of restoration. I constantly remind everyone we are a people business first and an automotive restoration company second. This is a novel and unique approach in our industry.

I recognize my greatest strength is getting people in the door. I am also confident in my team, knowing if I cannot answer a customer's question, I will be able to refer them to the right person.

With the good times, there have also been difficult times. It's difficult to make tough decisions. Recently, I had to deliver a difficult announcement about restructuring the business due to the slowed economy. I was concerned that making the wrong decision could crater the whole company. Plus, the number of hours you put into your business is incredible. As opposed to forty hours a week, you're there for eighty to one hundred hours a week. Another challenge of being the owner is that I am always reinvesting my income back into my business. Most of my employees take home much more than I do. In fact, I didn't even take a paycheck at all my entire first year as owner so we could get the company started on the right foot. So contrary to the misconception that people have about entrepreneurs, I am not in it to get rich overnight. I view this as an investment that will pay back in future years.

My recommendation to future entrepreneurs is to first draw up a business plan, consider your competition, and review the four Ps of marketing (product, price, place, and promotion) before beginning your business venture. Consider carefully who you are, what you are selling, who you are selling to, and what those customers need to know to be convinced to buy from you. Always put yourself in the customers' shoes.

I owe my success to having *passion*, doing what I love—restoring cars—implementing *excellent customer service*, and *having the right team*.

[Editor's note: Before publication, I learned Mr. Miller was forced to file for bankruptcy and close his business. Noting he had done so many things right, including identifying his target market, great customer service, quality work, and unique marketing, *and* was recognized as number 1202 on the Inc. 5000 list of the fastest-growing companies in America, I thought others could learn from his experience and asked if he would be willing to reflect on it. He graciously agreed; and without a doubt, you will learn and be inspired.]

I have lost none of my spirit despite the closing of our business and the hard economic times. I still believe starting and running your own company can be a good thing. I still have a positive outlook on business and life in general. What's done is done. Life is still good. I still have my wife, my family, my health, etc.

I had great fun taking Trinity from *zero* to $6 million in annual revenues in only five years. We are almost certain to make the Inc. 500 rather than the Inc. 5,000 this year based on our final year results in 2008, before we closed on December 16, 2008. That means we went from $1.6 million in 2006 to $3.4 million in 2007 to $6.2 million in 2008. We were in the top 1 percent of sales in our industry nationwide. Yes, the top 1 percent. We were huge. Wow!

For four years, it seemed we could do no wrong as a business; and everything we did just worked out for one reason or another, and I became a little cocky. This is *not* good. I didn't watch my pennies as well as all businesses should, small and large alike. As Ben Franklin once said, "Small leaks sink big ships." I spent a little too much on everything; and when times were good, we got away with it, but spending too much is a bad habit for any business. All businesses have to pinch their pennies in good times and in bad.

On top of this, I overextended our business and spent all our cash reserves getting into additional, noncore businesses like motorcycles and custom car construction. These used far more cash than they created. We should have stuck to our core businesses of paint, body, and mechanical and kept any extra money in the bank. All businesses should keep six months of gross sales in the bank as a reserve. Six months—that's a huge number and hard to save up, but it's necessary as a cushion against ups and downs and worse.

These are classic mistakes you can read about in business textbooks, but people still make them every day, so we *must* continue to harp on them year after year and hope a few business owners hear and listen. Then the worst came at the end of 2008 during the exact week I was in Washington DC accepting my Inc. 5,000 award. The economy took a 1929-size dump. I was standing on the stage in my tux, faking a smile for the cameras, and I knew we were done. The writing was on the wall, and I knew it—had known it in September of 2008. I put on a brave face and didn't say a word to anyone, especially to my parents, who were in Washington with me. It was awkward for me, but they didn't have a clue, and I didn't want to ruin our weekend together.

At home, I did my best to gather the troops and warn them things had to change. We cut spending on everything, we reduced staff to bare minimums, we brought in all the new customers we could, but nothing helped; our goose was cooked. Gross sales revenues were half of our breakeven as the economy declined.

We started missing our rent and loan payments. I tried to find investors to help. I tried to sell the business for the debt and walk away with nothing just so it would continue under new owners and the employees could keep their jobs. None of it worked. The economy was everyone's excuse. And they were right. It was bad. Everyone was hurting; no one was in the market to buy a company—not even a good company they really wanted. They just couldn't come up with the money. Several buyers pulled out at the last moment. The final one pulled out the morning of our planned closing in early December, and I knew we were done. I had been borrowing money to stay open, but no one would loan me another dime. I mortgaged everything, personal and professional, to stay afloat—another mistake, especially the personal part.

So I got the managers together and told them if we shut down right now, today, everyone would walk with a paycheck. There was just enough money in the bank account. If we went past the holidays, which everyone hoped we could do, the paychecks would bounce; and I didn't want to go out that way. It was the week before Christmas. The decision to close that day was tough, but it was the right one. So I gathered everyone together and told them the straight truth about our company situation.

Some were mad, most were sad, a few cried. It was the end of the dream. For a brief shining moment, we had created the best place to work in our industry nationwide, and everyone was very proud, especially me. I had the best people in the business, and it still humbles me they would follow my charge.

I'm proud of everything we accomplished. It's the people I'm going to miss, not the business or the money. I made more money in corporate America, but Trinity was so incredibly fun.

Trinity and my wife and I filed Chapter 7 bankruptcy on January 23, 2009. I have taken a day job and am moving forward with my life. I refuse to waste time being sad about Trinity. I treat it like a friend that has died. I only allow myself to think about the good times and just move forward. I think about the people and miss them every morning at eight o'clock when I don't see them as usual. Then I close my eyes, see their faces in mental snapshots of better times, smile, and go about my day, not knowing what the future holds but having faith that we'll all make lemonade out of the lemons of the current economy.

Entrepreneurs should hire a bookkeeper to say no, especially if they are crazy sales and marketing people like me. We shouldn't be anywhere near the company checkbook. I should have stayed at the front door, talking to customers. That was my best place in the company. Hopefully, I'll live and learn. That's my goal now. Guys like me are best with the top line, not the bottom line. You have to stick with what you're good at in life.

Now I'm back to sales and marketing, where I belong. And yes, my new employer has a bookkeeper to say no.

David Miller II
Contributed by Christina Ikard

KEY SUCCESS FACTORS: Passion, Customer Service, Customer Respect, Having the Right Team

RECOMMENDED BOOKS: *Good to Great* by Jim Collins, *Built to Last* by Jim Collins, most importantly, *It's Your Ship* by Michael Abrashoff

EDITOR'S NOTES: David W. Miller II grew up in Tulsa, Oklahoma, where he attended Hale High School. David was raised by his mom, who, as a struggling divorcee, raised two boys while holding down a full-time career in the telecommunications industry. She began her career as a secretary and retired as a director of the company. David says his mom is a tough lady and gave him the best advice of all: work hard every day, and never burn your bridges in life. He views his mom as his role model for these reasons and many others. After high school, David attended Oklahoma State University, where he received a BA in Industrial Organizational Psychology and Marketing in 1992. He finished his MBA in 2003.

David is happily married to Heather, whom he met while in college. She is co-owner of the Home Collection, a home décor and interior design business in the Utica Square Shopping Center in Tulsa, Oklahoma. David indicated Heather is his biggest fan and his worst critic. She is a very strong, determined woman who is not afraid of voicing her concerns about his ideas but stands behind him no matter what the outcome. She has been the love of his life for nineteen years.

CHAPTER EIGHT

IT'S ALL IN THE FAMILY

If you can give your son or daughter only one gift, let it be enthusiasm.
—Bruce Barton

That some achieve great success, is proof to all that others can achieve it as well.
—Abraham Lincoln

A THOUSAND DOLLARS AND A KITCHEN TABLE

This story was written as told by Callie Ketchum's grandmother, Betty Ketchum, and her father, Kevin Ketchum.

A thousand dollars, the hope of getting a loan, a kitchen table, and a smile on my face—this is how it all began. A true rags-to-riches story that required risk at the highest level. My family barely had enough to meet our needs as we struggled paycheck to paycheck. My four sons were raised in the roughest areas of New Orleans before we moved to Tulsa in 1975. The youngest was in eighth grade, and the oldest was a senior in high school, critical years for all of them. I decided to take a chance and risked it all. I knew I could sell pipe. I had worked for Bethlehem Steel for twenty years and knew the business well. When I landed in Tulsa, I had saved a thousand dollars of my moving money from Bethlehem. I had always been driven to work for myself, so when the opportunity came I was ready. I knew I had to risk big—really big—and take the chance to live my dream. I quit Bethlehem Steel, applied for a loan, and prayed for my dream to come true. I could never have imagined how big that dream would be.

I received my start through a $50,000 minority loan from Amoco Venture Capital. The loans were available for minorities, and as an American Indian, I qualified. I set up shop at our kitchen table in March of 1977 and Red Man Pipe and Supply was born. My wife, Betty, did the bookkeeping; and I worked on getting contracts with pipe companies and began selling pipe to drilling companies and oil and gas companies. I traveled constantly and worked extremely long hours to build my network and my business. We opened our first supply store in Ardmore, Oklahoma. I was lucky; and by the end of our first year, we were profitable. Fortunately, those were good years for the oil and gas industry, and I received large purchase orders from several companies.

The business continued to grow, and I hired more people, opened more supply stores, and continued stressing customer service. Business was thriving, and half of my employees had Native American tribal affiliation. I generously contributed to scholarship funds, truly believing education was key for the Indian people. I genuinely liked people, and they seemed to trust me. I felt the customer deserved to be treated well, and we were known for our excellent customer service. After five years in business, our spirits were soaring and so was our business. I felt on top of the world, with our gross volume being around $70 million. Not bad for a business that started at the kitchen table. Unfortunately, no one could have predicted the downswing in store for the oil industry.

In an effort to weather the downturn, I decided to move inventory by developing relationships with smaller independent companies instead of catering solely to larger companies. With oil down to $10 or less per barrel, we tightened the belt and put everything into our relationships. We did deals where we made pennies, but we moved pipe that kept our clients in business. It also strengthened their relationships with us. The goal was to survive. Our clients had to survive if we were to survive. We were all in this together, and survival was the only goal. Companies were going out of business everywhere, and I was scared. I could see the dream crumbling before my eyes.

During this time, I was elected Chief of the Delaware Tribe. It was 1983, and I was trying to keep my company afloat and lead a tribe through the hard times. It was the biggest challenge I had ever faced. I borrowed from banks just to make payroll and kept hanging on—barely. With good people at my side, we somehow managed to weather the downturn in the early to mid-'80s. Because of the strong relationships we had developed, we continued to grow while some of our competitors did not. I began buying out some of my competitors and wanted to acquire Superior Supply Company. I needed financing, but the bank was not eager to give the amount I needed because I already owed them money. I had hit a roadblock, but knew it was what we needed to do. I wasn't about to give up on the bank. I called for another meeting and threw every ounce of knowledge and confidence I had at the bankers. My biggest strength was always selling, and I could sell myself and my company. It worked. I persuaded them to back Red Man, and we acquired Superior Supply Company. This acquisition tripled our staff, and we grew from four field stores to twenty-two—David had beaten Goliath.

In 1987, I received a very prestigious award from President Ronald Reagan, the National Minority Entrepreneur of the Year Award, in a formal ceremony in Washington DC. My entrepreneurial spirit had not gone unnoticed. As a very humble Native American, I was quite honored. You see, I've always believed good wins out. You work hard, you treat people right, it comes back to you; and that award proved my thinking was correct. The award drove me to do more. Our company was successful, and we gave back to the community that supported us. We gave generously to the United Way and the American Heart Association. We also increased our scholarship funding. We had become well known in Tulsa and sponsored as many events as we could afford. We always kept expenses at a minimum, worked hard, hired just enough to get by, and expected the best from employees. My family continued to live quite frugally. They were used to living on virtually nothing and that changed very little. Our employees were like extended family members. We were a private business striving to grow.

In 1995, my hope of entering the downstream market became a reality when we acquired Vinson Supply Company's PVF division. This enabled us to become one of only two suppliers with the capability to service its clients both upstream and downstream. We created superstores and assets included fifty-five thousand products throughout a network of fifty-five locations. Red Man had truly become the supplier of choice. My dream was complete—the company was booming and all my sons were in the business working in their particular niche. I was a happy man and humbled by my success.

My success was attributable to several factors. I was fortunate to be likeable, and I could sell products because people liked and trusted me. My family always thought I was someone with true charisma. Maybe it was true, but I would say it was simply that I treated others like I wanted to be treated. I also worked hard and never gave up. I had a never-quit attitude and would do anything a customer needed. The customer was first and right about everything. As I have always said, relationships in life, whether business or personal, are the most important things to build. Money is definitely not the driver, and was never the driver for me. I lived a very rich life through my relationships and was a very happy and contented man.

Lewis B. Ketchum
Contributed by Callie Ketchum

KEY SUCCESS FACTORS: Vision, Customer Service Orientation, Perseverance, Strong Communication Skills, Ability To Sell/Persuade Others, Belief in What is Right, Always Doing the Right Thing.

WEB SITE: *www.mcjunkinredman.com*

EDITOR'S NOTES: Lew Ketchum died in September 1995 from heart failure. His funeral gave tribute to the charismatic man he was, with more attendees than anyone had ever seen in the large church. It was so full people stood in the hallways. People traveled from all over to attend, some from as far away as Greece. He was one of those people whom everyone liked and respected. He always did the right thing and trusted people. He was truly an amazing man.

Lew's oldest son, Craig, was not prepared to take over the company, but was forced forced to do so upon his father's death. He became President and CEO. Kent Ketchum ran the sales force out of Houston, Texas; Brian Ketchum ran the valve-fitting business; and Kevin managed the facility and vehicle leases and purchases. Each of the four sons stepped up to keep their father's dream alive. Each of them had their own individual niche, and they worked together to help the company survive without their father. Lew had raised his sons right. There was never any jealousy between them. Each made different salaries based on his contribution, not based on who they were. They all worked hard and did their specific part to keep the company growing . . . and it continued to grow. In 1999, the company was named the number one Minority Business in the nation; and in 2000, received the U.S. Department of Commerce MBDA Regional Award for Outstanding Commitment to Excellence.

In 2007, Goldman Sachs approached the family about purchasing Red Man Pipe and Supply in order to merge it with McJunkin—a competitor they had recently purchased. That sale took place, and the company is now known as McJunkin Red Man owned by Goldman Sachs. The joint company should go public sometime in 2009.

Lew Ketchum never imagined how big his risk would pay off. The company had annual sales of approximately $2 billion when Goldman Sachs purchased it.

Callie's sister recently decided to start her own business. She has a picture of their grandpa on her office wall. Callie said her grandpa would have smiled and said exactly what her parents said: "Build your dream, girls. If you believe in it, you will make it happen."

Train your head and hands to do, your head and heart to dare.

— *Joseph Cotter*

FAMILY FIRST

Being a man who always loved being around family, it was difficult living nine hundred miles away from my extended family when both my sons were born.

I was raised in Lakeland, Florida. From 2000 until 2007, I lived in Washington DC with my wife, Cherie. I enjoyed living in Washington DC, but I didn't want my sons to grow up in a city of that size. We thought it would be good for our sons to grow up close to their grandparents, so when Cherie was offered a job in Tampa, the move home to Lakeland felt like a natural choice.

Now I was suddenly living close to my parents, and unemployed. The big question for me was, what will I do? My brother Luke and I had always dreamed of opening our own business, but we never knew what kind of business. After spending seven years working for other people in Washington DC, I felt now would be the perfect time to finally be my own boss. Since my brother lived in Lakeland too, I pushed hard for us to bring our dream to reality. My brother liked the idea of starting a business, so the next step was to figure out what kind of business. After a lot of brainstorming and researching of the Lakeland area, we saw a need for a good golf store. All the golf stores in Lakeland had either failed or were not doing well. This fact did not scare us. We knew the demand for golf products in this area of the country was huge, and we could identify some of the problems that made the other stores fail. We would not repeat those errors. The move to Lakeland was about being in the right place at the right time.

Since neither my brother nor I had ever owned our own business, we needed a lot of advice. After looking at numerous options, we felt starting a franchise would probably be the best for us. Golf Etc had a main focus on fitting and repairing clubs, and we felt this was in-line with what we wanted. It was also what earlier stores in Lakeland had missed. The other two things we found when researching why golf stores had failed were location and not having quality products in stock. The research we conducted was one of the best steps we took as entrepreneurs.

The store has only been open for a year. The start was tough, the days were really long, we spent a lot of time away from our families, and the profits were not as high as we would have liked.

We learned how to put our schedules together, and even though we still spend many long days in the store, our families are our highest priority. The store is doing really well, and we have a great reputation in Lakeland and the surrounding areas. I was determined that this was what I wanted to do, whether or not it made me wealthy.

Since the start a year ago, we have not had any big failures. We borrowed all the capital to open the store from our dad. I think this has helped us run the store during the first year, without feeling the stress of having to bring in profits in the short run to be able to pay the bank. We have been able to run our store with more of a long-term focus.

I believe the key to our success is our location. As the research showed us, the location can make or break a retail store. Our store is in a relatively new outdoor mall area, an area that already had restaurants, clothing stores, a cinema, and hotels. This mall is the place to be in Lakeland, and we were extremely happy we could open our store here and be a part of it. Many of our customers would never drive to a golf store that was isolated. However, in the mall, they can combine shopping in other stores with a trip to Golf Etc®.

From day one, our goal was to differentiate ourselves from previous golf stores in the area. The biggest challenge we are facing now is that golfers in Lakeland have become accustomed to having to drive to either Tampa or Orlando. They do not even consider the possibility of finding a store in Lakeland that can serve their needs. Considering our store has been open for only a year, this situation should change with time. The next step for me as an entrepreneur is to find ways to attract every golfer from this area to visit our store. I have placed ads in local papers, magazines, and on the radio. I believe, however, the best advertising is word of mouth. If we do our best at pleasing our existing customers, they will come back and bring additional customers with them. We will continue to give back to the community by sponsoring local golf tournaments. These sponsorships are also a perfect opportunity to advertise the store.

What I have learned as an entrepreneur is as long as you do something to set yourself apart from your competitors, and you are determined, you have a great chance for success. No matter how important your business is for you, never prioritize your business higher than your family. Your family will be there to support you at all times, while the business is "only" money.

JJ Miller
Contributed by Pernilla Lindberg

KEY SUCCESS FACTORS: Location, Determination, Goal Orientation

RECOMMENDED BOOKS: *The Winners Manual: For the Game of Life* by Jim Tressel, Chris Fabry, and John Maxwell

WEB SITE: *www.golfetclakeland.com*

EDITOR'S NOTES: JJ Miller is married to Cherie Miller, and they have two sons, Jake and Nate. JJ and Cherie met in Nashville, Tennessee, where they both went to college. When the Miller family has some spare time, they drive to Disney World in Orlando and spend a couple of hours there. The whole family has season passes to Disney World they use as much as possible.

Your living is determined not so much by what life brings to you as by what you bring to life.
—John Homer Miller

CAPPUCCINO WITH A HEART

Izola, Slovenia, a small European town on the Slovene coast, is lively with people who have fallen in love with the sea. Traditional fishing, shipbuilding, and a newly built marina provide a warm and charming atmosphere, which entices visitors to return.

Born in Izola, my life has been different from that of my parents, who grew up in the former Yugoslavia. My dad was a sailor, and my mother was employed in horticulture, working with flowers. I lived a happy life with a loving family, but entrepreneurship was not an option for my parents.

Six years ago, at the age of twenty-six, I left my job to give birth to our first child, a beautiful baby girl. I have a strong work ethic, so every place I had been employed promised to hire me again when I was ready to return. But when the time came, the jobs were not available! In the face of this dilemma, my husband and my mother encouraged me to become an entrepreneur and have my own business. It was something I desired to do but for which there was no money, so I approached a bank for a loan—and was turned down. I went to the second bank and was fortunate to be given a €5,000 credit line.

Subsequently, I purchased *caffe alle porte*, a traditional coffee shop that was struggling to survive. The challenge was to make changes so customers enjoyed being there and were sure to return, so the business would be profitable. My goal was to provide an upscale atmosphere, offering the clientele a great experience and a choice of drinks including high-quality coffee, cappuccino, and café latte. I looked at my competition and planned the changes needed to operate a competitive business. My former employment and experience in similar businesses was beneficial. With passion and perseverance, I turned *caffe alle porte* into a bustling business, where local customers and tourists love the experience and return with their friends. Like the story title implies, each cup of cappuccino is served with a heart!

Some of the changes necessary to make *caffe alle porte* successful were simple, and some were more difficult. Changes included serving higher-quality coffee; adding products such as soft drinks, fresh-squeezed juices, beer, and alcoholic drinks; and remodeling the décor to provide a charming European atmosphere.

More challenging were replacing the employees so customer service would be superb and attracting a desirable clientele. The culture *had* to be different, and sometimes this meant asking customers who abused alcohol, as well as those who made other customers feel uncomfortable, to leave and not return. In the early stages of the business, the people aspect—including employees and customers—was the most critical and challenging. Just like a good cappuccino, the ingredients for a successful business are complex.

The first year was the most difficult, with most of the money going back to the bank and only enough left over for the essentials. The second year was also a challenge; but by the third year, business was good. We are now in our sixth year, with ten employees and a great business!

Slovenia has extremely strict laws for businesses: laws that include inspections for cleanliness, type and volume of music, how products are displayed, posting of prices, size requirements for signs, itemized bill delivered to customer prior to payment, etc. Sometimes inspectors visit your business without your knowing why they are there. Failure to comply with the laws may result in a fine of €10,000. Although inspections are designed to ensure quality, having to be aware of and adhere to the numerous rules and regulations puts added stress on business owners.

Two years after buying *caffe alle porte*, my husband, Robert Sterpin, and I purchased a second business, Bora Sport Group, which offers skiing, mountain hiking, bicycling, and sailing equipment and clothing, as well as other sports-related items. When we acquired the business, only two brands were offered. We now offer fifteen brands, including products from Italy, Germany, and Sweden. Annual sales recently exceeded €1 million, and our goal is to triple that within the next three years. Our retail store is in Izola, and our wholesale operation includes sales to Slovenia, Serbia, Croatia, Bosnia, and Montenegro. We are now designing our own brand, Bora Performance, which will be available in the next year. Robert takes responsibility for the day-to-day operations of this business, and I manage most of the paperwork and accounting activities.

My biggest accomplishments as an entrepreneur are not in the money I earn but in the rewards I feel by creating jobs for others, providing customers with a place to enjoy cappuccino or other drinks with friends, and having the flexibility being my own boss provides.

My advice to an entrepreneur is to find a niche in which you have a particular interest, have a passion for what you do, understand the financial aspects of the business, and know you will work many more than eight hours a day. With these things in mind, being an entrepreneur can be exciting and rewarding. And if you love what you are doing, it is not really work!

Tamara Dujmovic

KEY SUCCESS FACTORS: Calculated Passion, Work Ethic, Feeling Good About What You Do

WEB SITES: *www.caffe-alle-porte.bora.si, www.bora.si*

EDITOR'S NOTES: Tamara lives with her husband, Robert, and two children in Izola, Slovenia. She enjoys traveling and skiing in Slovenia, Italy, Austria, and France. Future plans for Tamara and her family include visits to the United States and Canada.

On the Adriatic coast of the Istrian Peninsula, Izola has a Mediterranean atmosphere and is home to the only Slovene shipyard and fish-canning factory. More recently, its inhabitants have turned toward tourism, which is supported by the large marina.

Prior to 1991, Izola was part of the former Yugoslavia, and being an entrepreneur there was not possible. Slovenia was the first former Yugoslav republic to join the European Union, applying in 1996 and becoming a member in 2004.

There is a real magic in enthusiasm. It spells the difference between mediocrity and accomplishment.
—*Norman Vincent Peale*

WHEN THE WATER FLOWS, SO DOES THE CASH

How does being retired at the age of fifty-five sound? I think it sounds great! I own a commercial plumbing business—no, not the type of plumbing where I come to your house and dig in your toilet. I actually deal strictly with new construction. I began working for my father at age seventeen during the summers while I was still in high school. I went to college to become a stockbroker and graduated with a degree in finance and banking. But that plan fell through quickly. I decided I did not like the idea of working in an office and dreamed of being outdoors.

I became interested in commercial plumbing early in my college career. It was something that came easy for me, and I had seen the success my father was enjoying. My father, Don Redding, is a successful mechanical contractor who has been in business for over twenty-five years. Dad's company, Trademark Mechanical, has been extremely profitable and focuses strictly on commercial plumbing. I am not saying I immediately knew this was the business for me, but I caught on very quickly. I worked for my father for several years before realizing I wanted to own my own company. When I was thirty-two, after long discussions with my wife, I realized the time was right. My father had always been good to me, but I wanted to be my own boss.

Since I had been working for my father for several years, I had endless networking possibilities, which helped me to start bidding jobs. I was fortunate to have a father who helped me tremendously in getting my company, Midwest Mechanical Inc., started. Since I was going into the same business, my father helped me by bidding jobs in the name of Midwest instead of Trademark. I also established good credit and was able to get my own funding for Midwest with lines of credit from the bank. My father and his partner joined forces to help me begin Midwest, and having established supplier credit helped greatly in getting supplies and material.

With the tremendous effort by me, my wife, and my father, Midwest Mechanical became official in 2000. In its first year of business, Midwest Mechanical Inc. brought in $250,000 in revenue. There were only two employees: my wife and me. My wife, Robyn, helped with our accounting and the books for the company. Since I did not have employees yet, my father generously loaned me employees until I could afford to hire my own. Today Midwest is bringing in 2.5 million dollars in revenue, and I currently have around twenty employees. We have grown tremendously, considering the work depends on the demand. The state of the economy could cause trouble for Midwest because all of our work is new construction. Unfortunately, several jobs have been put on hold due to the liquidity crisis with the banking system. But I have faith in my company, and I believe we can overcome anything the economy puts in front of us.

The biggest internal challenge I have faced in my company was a job that went wrong. After Midwest worked on a job for two years, the company was unable to pay what it owed. Times became difficult because of the size of the job. I remember weeks when I would tell my wife not to cash our paychecks because there was not enough money in the account to cover them. Another reason we did not cash our checks was that I always put my employees first. I would rather not cash my paycheck and have enough to pay them so they can feed their families. There is no doubt overcoming this challenge has strengthened Midwest. We will continue to grow and progress even though we face setbacks.

I always try to give back to my community as much as I can. I am very proud of the donations we make. Midwest currently donates to Oklahoma Highway Patrol, Christian radio stations, Clarehouse Hospice, and the sports leagues in which our employees' children are involved. My wife's sister passed away two years ago, and the loving people at Clarehouse Hospice did everything they could to make our family feel comfortable. It is an extremely amazing company that survives solely off donations, and I will always do the best I can to help them. I am also proud I have never laid off employees. By providing jobs, I am also giving back to the community. These are hard times, and jobs are often difficult to get.

I have had great success with my company throughout the years. Failures at Midwest were jobs that went wrong, but the successes have overcome these failures. I am currently in the process of buying my father's company. We just finished building our new shop and office. Things could not be better! Trademark Mechanical, my father's company, will be merged with Midwest Mechanical. This is by far the biggest success in my career. I am forty-five years old and run a successful commercial plumbing business. I have a healthy wife and daughter who support me in everything I do, which ultimately means the world to me.

In ten years, I hope to be retired, with a house on the lake. I feel I have worked extremely hard to be where I am today. But without the supportive people in my life, I might never have made it. I know if I can succeed, then anyone can.

James Redding
Contributed by Jamie Thompson

KEY SUCCESS FACTORS: Work Ethic, Perseverance, Family Support

RECOMMENDED BOOKS: *Art of War* by Sun Tzu

EDITOR'S NOTES: James Redding lives in Coweta, Oklahoma, with his wife, Robyn Redding. They started their business in 2000. James enjoys watching OU football in his spare time. During the summers, he spends his time with his family at the lake. James has one daughter who is in college at Oklahoma State University.

The future is not a gift—it is an achievement.
—Harry Lauder

A GLOBAL ENTREPRENEUR

Imagine a place in Western Europe where you wake each morning to the snowcapped Swiss Alps to your west and Austria to your east. You are surrounded by the most beautiful natural scenes on earth. Yet you choose to leave such a place to study mechanical engineering and automotive design at Wismar Engineering College in Germany.

This may be a pretty common occurrence today, but this story begins in 1941, at the start of the most devastating war in the history of the world, World War II. Western Europe during this time was an extremely hostile place. How would someone at the age of twenty-six start his own company during this time and succeed? But not only did the company succeed, it grew into a global company operating in 120 countries, employing over twenty-one thousand people worldwide, with more than 4.7 billion Swiss francs in sales annually—landing the owner's family on the Forbes World's Richest People list in 2005. This entire process started in a family garage in Schaan, Liechtenstein, a country that is only sixty-two square miles.

Martin Hilti traveled back to Liechtenstein after studying mechanical engineering and automotive design in college. He and his brother Eugen set up a small mechanical workshop in their garage under the name Maschinenbau Hilti OHG and set out to find contract work from the German automotive industry. The company grew to more than one hundred employees, making components and products based on other engineers' designs. The company was successful but still small at the end of World War II. The only problem was that with the collapse of Germany, their entire customer base was dismantled. This major setback forced the brothers to look for a new customer base. Martin turned his attention to the Swiss textile industry, which was rapidly expanding at this time. The next decade saw Hilti's tremendous success in the textile industry in Switzerland; and in 1952, the company expanded into Italy, the first of their many international expansions. The Hiltis were still manufacturing goods based on other engineers' designs, and Martin and his brother were eager to design and develop a product of their own.

At the end of the 1940s, Martin began to look into the power tool industry. He saw a design for a tool that would make it possible for a worker to shoot threaded nails into concrete and steel. These threaded nails could then be used to attach machinery. Martin was so interested that he purchased the design and patent for the tool. Martin and Eugen spent several years refining the design to make it safer and began selling their product under the name of Perfix.

Little did they know this tool would revolutionize the world's construction industry. They continued to improve on the design and eventually added a trigger-firing system with black powder cartridges to fire the tool. This addition made the tool much like a gun and very easy for the everyday worker to use. But the tools could shoot a nail just like a bullet and were very dangerous on job sites. So Martin developed a piston-firing system that greatly reduced the velocity of the fastener and added seven other safety measures to the tool. Martin Hilti had become the father of the low velocity powder actuated fastening system. The safety features removed the threat that the nail would travel out of the gun like a bullet, and construction companies around the world clamored to get their hands on this newer and safer product.

In 1954, the Hilti brothers renamed the Perfix product with their family name; and by 1957, the redesigned tool, the Hilti DX 100, was available to the market. This tool made Hilti an everyday name on construction sites and launched a global company. Its success led to the company's expansion into Sweden, Ireland, England, South Africa, Peru, and the United States. Eugen Hilti passed away in 1964, and Martin Hilti assumed full responsibility for Hilti, which had been set up as a limited liability corporation in 1960. By then, the Hilti Corporation had removed itself from the textile industry and was focused 100 percent on the professional power tools market. The company stayed true to its roots of research and development and began refining designs to create safer and more productive tools.

Hilti began to develop multiple tool lines, and the company is now involved in the product line of every major tool used by the construction industry. Martin had focused on developing more efficient and safer tools in an industry where injury was just part of the job, and the company is still on the cutting edge of the design of safer products. Hilti Corporation has developed drills that sense when the operator is in danger and shuts off automatically, laser measuring systems used by first responders, and diamond-sawing systems used by firefighters in traffic collisions. The company also provides on-the-job safety training to a client's employees. Its advanced research of construction materials to make them safer and stronger has revolutionized the construction industry, but perhaps the most important contribution has been the developments in firestopping technology. Hilti is dedicated to the fire protection industry and employs a full staff of firestopping engineers that provide professional consulting to contractors and inspectors free of charge on-site, online, and over the phone. Firestopping systems in buildings help contain fires and keep smoke from spreading, giving people in the building more time to evacuate. This technology has saved thousands of lives over the last twenty years.

Mr. Hilti has passed on, but the company is now under the guidance of his son, Michael Hilti. Martin had never envisioned developing a company that would someday save lives around the world. He was an entrepreneur who was sure he could use his engineering background to improve on modern designs and make safer and more efficient products for his customers. He faced a unique challenge by building a company in the midst of World War II and being successful. Mr. Hilti showed his ability to adapt and overcome when his entire customer base was erased with the collapse of Germany. He was able to refocus his business for a different country and a completely different industry. Mr. Hilti's passion to create and innovate led to the global revolution of an entire industry and has created a safer environment for millions of construction employees.

Martin Hilti
Contributed by Brian Inman

KEY SUCCESS FACTORS: Passion, Adaptability, Taking Action, Work Ethic, Focus

WEB SITE: *www.hilti.com*

EDITOR'S NOTES: Hilti is a global leader of value-added, top-quality products for professional customers in the construction and building-maintenance industries. The company was recognized in the December 2008 issue of *Harvard Business Review* for being on the cutting edge of innovation.

CHAPTER NINE

KNOWLEDGE THROUGH EXPERIENCE

Knowledge is the frontier of tomorrow.
—*Dennis Waitley*

When a man is willing and eager, the gods join in.
—Aeschylus

THINGS THEY NEVER TELL YOU ABOUT OWNING YOUR OWN BUSINESS

When I was a kid, I had a Kool-Aid stand, organized the neighborhood circus, and had a paper route. As I grew older, I worked in a grocery store and shoe store to make money. While in college, I started a laundry service, taking other kids' dirty laundry to the cleaners, who, in exchange, did my laundry for free.

After college, while I was teaching school, I started a small advertising and marketing company to earn money to pay back my college loans and started writing articles for local newspapers, giving speeches, and just about anything else I could do to make a few extra bucks. As a result of writing a letter to a local TV station criticizing the news staff for not spending more time on business and money news, I wound up with a job as one of the nation's first business and economics editors and, subsequently, a news anchor. I did all of this while continuing to attend college to earn my master's and doctoral degrees.

My advertising agency work grew and eventually led me to another job—as VP of Marketing for a restaurant company, which led me to start my own restaurant business. Eateries Inc. grew from an idea to one Garfield's Restaurant, to a chain of over fifty Garfield's Restaurants, to include Pepperoni Grill and Garcia's Mexican Restaurants.

Given all of this, I guess it's safe to say I'm an entrepreneur. I knew early in life I preferred leading over following. I wanted to be in charge rather than have others in charge of me. I was willing to take risks, preferring to focus on what was achievable rather than worry about failure.

I never thought about how much I had to work. As long as I enjoyed what I was doing and was in charge, it didn't matter whether it was a few hours' work or the typical ten- to twelve-hour day. I was willing to invest, spend my own money, and go without getting paid for a long time, but never felt it wasn't worth the effort. On the contrary, like many entrepreneurs, we believe we can do it all . . . whatever it takes to conquer the challenge.

Like many successful entrepreneurs, I knew enough about what I didn't know and was smart enough to surround myself with people who were good at what I wasn't. I asked a lot of questions, trying to avoid mistakes others had made doing the same things I was about to do. Because my company was small, I realized I would spend hours doing things that were not my strengths because there was no one else to do them. I learned about negotiating leases, insurance, taking our company public, dealing with SEC regulations—and then there was the lawsuit. A supplier sent us contaminated food and nearly bankrupted one of our restaurant chains. I spent five years focused on rebuilding a division of our company, which kept me from focusing on the parts that were successful. We filed a lawsuit that cost us over $1 million and tens of thousands of hours of work. We won our suit and a sizeable award, but the money didn't make up for the lost time and momentum and the damaged reputation. I learned managing a company trying not to fail is different from managing a company trying to succeed.

No books or lectures can ever prepare you to own your own business. No matter how much you read, how many stories you hear, and how much advice you get, nothing teaches you more than being in business for yourself. Eateries Inc. grew to become a nationally recognized chain of dinner-house restaurants that reached from California to New York. We employed over three thousand people, and our annual sales exceeded $100 million. I had the honor of being the president and CEO of that company for twenty-two years.

I always enjoyed my work, but as we grew larger, I began to see fewer and fewer of our employees. Part of the fun for me was being a small start-up company, where I could mentor the younger people around me. Watching them succeed was more rewarding than the success I was enjoying.

One of the mistakes many entrepreneurs make is to grow beyond their capability. People often ask if I was sad to sell the company. The answer is no. I achieved a dream, a fair amount of success, some financial rewards, and helped several others succeed as well. That's a pretty good business.

Vince Orza

KEY SUCCESS FACTORS: Work Ethic, Learning From Your Mistakes, Taking Risks

RECOMMENDED BOOKS: *Good to Great* by Jim Collins, *Iacocca: An Autobiography* by Lee Iacocca, *Failure Is Not an Option: Mission Control from Mercury to Apollo 13 and Beyond* by Gene Kranz

EDITOR'S NOTES: The dynamic career of Dr. Vince Orza includes being a television news anchor, corporate executive, entrepreneur, university professor, dean, and two-time candidate for governor. Dr. Orza says he has learned more from failure than success, and as you can see from his story, he has been blessed with much-deserved success.

If you want to be truly successful, invest in yourself to get the knowledge you need to find your unique factor. When you find it and focus on it and persevere, your success will blossom.

—Sidney Madweb

FROM NO STREET TO WALL STREET

Growing up on a farm family, we were always at risk. Not knowing anything different, I just thought that was life. I started my own agricultural business while still in high school. As simple as it was, it kept what small capital I had invested in growing cotton and buying calves. I was buying appreciating assets, not cars. The most I ever invested was a couple of thousand dollars, which was mostly borrowed.

My first exposure to entrepreneurship came when I went to Wall Street, where I learned about investments. I was twenty-four years old, and this was my first exposure to capitalism. Speculation and lending were rampant. Big risks were being taken everywhere—big cars, Rolex watches, big houses, and big lifestyles. Then it happened; the bottom fell out. Oklahoma lost over one hundred banks in the early 1980s. The state went into a recession that lasted over a decade. This event affected every person in Oklahoma. We bet everything on the boom and lost it all in the bust.

Fast-forward to 1993. Several friends and I decided to open a broker-dealer in Oklahoma City with a focus on helping Oklahoma-based businesses raise money and helping our local economy out of the doldrums. In May of 1995, we opened Capital West Securities. Having purchased the Oklahoma and Texas offices of an already-operating NYSE company, we were off and running from day one. However, during the first year, we made just about every mistake in the book. By the end of the first year, we had to recapitalize, step back, and look at our business plan. It was flawed. We were trying to be all things to all people, not realizing we had to focus our efforts on what we did best. We restructured and turned Capital West into a very successful business. If you were successful in bringing profitable business into the firm, you got paid. This policy gave each of us unlimited income potential. It also gave each of us equal risk. As the economy changed and our income fluctuated, we all faced the same challenges. Since taking this attitude and business philosophy, we have not had a losing year. One of the main lessons I learned through this experience was to not get overburdened with debt.

The thrill has been seeing Oklahoma, and especially Oklahoma City, change. We've had some great firms begin here with a simple idea and grow into the largest in their field. These CEOs have been in the forefront of giving back to the community through both time and money. Our civic leaders have had the foresight and fortitude to take risks to bring our city back from virtually nothing to where it is now.

My personal philosophy and, I believe, the reason for much of my success, has been to demonstrate hard work, utilize the value of networking, be involved, and enjoy what I am doing. Other than these values, I think one of the things that has helped me was the timing of forming our business. In the mid-1990s, Oklahoma was coming into a time of prosperity. We had civic and business leaders who were willing to take chances. Oklahoma City had started projects that some thought would never work, but they did work beyond our wildest expectations.

Another important thing is the ability to get the name of your company "branded." In other words, when you first start your own adventure, you will be asked, "Who do you work for? What do you do?" You need to work very hard to get your name out so it is widely known. This takes time, money, and getting involved; but in the end, being a brand name gives you the credibility you need to succeed.

Because we had help along the way, it's important to give back. Being involved in your local chamber, state chamber, local civic clubs, charities, and anything else you might deem important will pay off professionally, as well as give you personal satisfaction beyond your expectations. I have observed along the way that the most successful people seem to be the busiest people, those giving back the most. No excuses.

I think the following advice is important to long-term success:

1. Never put your integrity at risk. The temptation will someday come. Don't take the easy way. Remember, if it looks too good to be true, something may be wrong.
2. Stay current on events around you. Read and observe. Things are always changing, and you need to be aware.
3. If you want to know how a person thinks, read the person's biography (Suggestion: Boone Pickens).
4. One of the easiest ways to test your idea is, "Would I write a check for this product?"
5. Have fun.

One of the best things about being an entrepreneur is there is no limit to what you can accomplish; you have unlimited potential! The only problem with being an entrepreneur is having the ability to take risks and not let the highs and lows bother you. Is it worth it? I believe so.

Bob Rader

KEY SUCCESS FACTORS: Integrity, Work Ethic, Branding

RECOMMENDED BOOKS: *NUTS! Southwest Airlines' Crazy Recipe for Business and Personal Success* by Kevin and Jackie Freiberg, *Memos from the Chairman* by Alan C. "Ace" Greenberg

WEB SITE: *www.capitalwest.com*

EDITOR'S NOTES: Bob and Judy Rader met at and graduated from Oklahoma State University. Judy was from Tulsa, and Bob from El Reno. Living in Oklahoma City for over forty-five years, they are passionate about the success and future of Oklahoma, especially Oklahoma City. Seeing all the good things that have happened, and their involvement in Oklahoma City, they can't imagine living elsewhere.

Formal education will make you a living. Self-education will make you a fortune.
—Jim Rohn

ONE SIMPLE BEGINNING TO THREE EXTRAORDINARY CAREERS

Born to immigrants in a small Kansas town, I understood early on what hard work meant. My father owned a small store, which gave me my first glimpse into entrepreneurship. I understood entrepreneurs were people who work sixteen hours a day for themselves to prevent having to work eight hours for someone else.

I always knew I'd be an entrepreneur, but I made a necessary detour just after I finished high school. When I was eighteen, I joined the Army and served for three years in response to Pearl Harbor. My three years in the Army were probably the best thing that ever happened to me, because I was able to use the GI Bill to attend Oklahoma State University. In 1946, I began studying Accounting. By 1949, I had finished my Bachelor's Degree at OSU and a Master's Degree at Northwestern.

But my education didn't stop there. I've been a student of business for over fifty years. In 1949, I began teaching Accounting at Wichita State University. I was a member of the Accounting faculty for forty years, serving as Dean of the College of Business for seven. In 1964, when I began my tenure as dean, our school grew considerably. Mostly, the growth occurred because WSU was transitioning from being funded as a municipal university to being funded as a state university. Four years into my tenure as dean, we reached AACSB accreditation, the highest accreditation for schools of business. I stepped down from being dean in 1971, but had many more years to serve the university.

In 1977, I changed my focus at the university. Entrepreneurship was a new field, and I wanted to explore the possibilities. At first, our dean agreed to a summer workshop program, but I had to find the funding for the workshop from outside the College of Business. I had some business contacts from my consulting and was able to find the funding in the Wichita community. We had a wonderful group of students, and our success sparked the first Center for Entrepreneurship in the nation. It wasn't easy to gain support for our program, especially as a part of the business college. Many traditional members of academia opposed the addition of entrepreneurship to colleges of business. Perhaps it does contain less theory than other subjects, but it is a wonderful way to bring all of those theories together to create something tangible. Changing from teaching accounting to focusing on entrepreneurship was exciting. My biggest thrill has always been to learn something new. Many people from small towns are like that—they want to dream big and to have the tools to achieve what they have dreamed. I saw a way for entrepreneurship to give them those tools.

Since 1977, our university's program has matured and is one of the best entrepreneurship programs in the nation. It was a wonderful experience to help start the program. Throughout my teaching career, I had been consulting for businesses and enjoyed teaching students about my consulting experiences with business owners.

When I left in 1989, I decided I was not finished learning. My son, Harvey, and I created Jabara Ventures Group. It's a venture capital company that invests in companies. We've also worked with many entrepreneurs. Our advice to any entrepreneur is the four *S*s: stop spending, start saving. We don't own any entities by ourselves, but we own parts of many ventures. We deal with many different types of entities, which is where my CPA certification is helpful.

A few years after starting Jabara Ventures Group, we decided to start VentureKids. VentureKids is dedicated to teaching minority fifth graders about entrepreneurship. The young students who participate in our program receive a $50 savings bond and are encouraged to see how much they can make it grow. It's a wonderful way to help them learn how to apply what they've learned.

We've also been involved in the community in other ways, but I've never seen it as a sacrifice. The community is important to all of us—it's not a sacrifice to help your community; it's an expectation. Specifically, when I was dean, I was expected to be involved in several aspects of our community. And it wasn't always giving money to a cause or attending an event. Service also included recommending my best students to industry employers and being involved in community activities.

I was a professor for forty years, a business consultant for over forty years, and an entrepreneur for over forty years. Some say that's why I look like I'm 120 years old. Since leaving the university, people have asked me when I plan to retire. I simply ask them what they'd have me do instead of continuing to be an entrepreneur and consultant. I work six days a week, and I enjoy every minute of it. My son is involved with our business as well, so it's a family venture. If you find something you love and make it your career, you won't mind working every day.

People often ask me about challenges I've had to overcome—I can't think of one. Every time I've had a challenge, I've mapped a strategy for overcoming it. There is opportunity in everything. Sometimes it's getting out and trying something new; other times, it's figuring out how to get out of a situation. I've had the opportunity to develop relationships with businesspeople in the Wichita community. Even though I've retired from teaching, the opportunities to share what I do with others continue.

I've had a wonderful life. When people ask if I would change anything, I answer no. I have three wonderful children, three wonderful grandchildren, and a wife who kept it all going. Even when I was dean, my wife managed two young daughters, a house, and the role of dean's wife. I have had a lot of experiences. I think you have to find the opportunity in everything. Success is available in whatever decision you make, you just have to find where and how.

Fran Jabara
Contributed by Mary Marshall

KEY SUCCESS FACTORS: Knowing Your Competition, Work Ethic, Being Financially Responsible

EDITOR'S NOTES: Fran Jabara and his wife, Geri, live in Wichita, Kansas. Fran continues to work six days a week with his son at Jabara Ventures Group. They remain active in the Wichita community and continue to provide support to both Oklahoma State University and Wichita State University. Professor Jabara's passion is sharing his love of entrepreneurship with students.

Intellectual capital is the most valuable of all factors of production.
—*Brian Tracy*

RULES FOR LIFE AS AN ENTREPRENEUR

I started to work right out of college with Shell Oil Company because they had the best training program. That's when I established rule number one: work for the best. After eight years, I had the opportunity to run the exploration and producing division for a small company in Houston, Associated Oil & Gas. There I learned much more about the business. We were successful because it was 1964, during the depths of the oil field depression, and I was able to hire outstanding talent. This is when I found rule number two: hire people smarter than you are. They'll make you look good. After two years of the poor economy in the oil and gas business, I lost my job.

I had always wanted to have my own business. My father and my mother were entrepreneurial, and that's probably where I got my desire. So now, without a job, I was an entrepreneur. Rule number three: have a nest egg. I had saved some $16,000, and that enabled me to maintain my family's standard of living and provided capital to run my oil and gas business. The best advice I received was, "Decide what you are going to do, and don't do anything else." Therefore, rule number four: make a carefully considered decision based on your talents and resources and stay focused.

My first prospect took a year and resulted in a dry hole. The second year, I got a tip from a friend, and hit a new oil field. We kept a reversionary interest after field payout, so we received no income for four years. I still had my nest egg but decided I didn't have enough capital to sustain an operation. So I took a job in Tulsa, running an exploration and production operation, LVO Corporation. Rule number five: raise enough capital to stay in business. This usually means you have to give up a share of your business. I had found Hope Field in Lavaca County, Texas and got the new job because of contacts I had made in college and through my first two jobs. That brings up rule number six: establish a network of successful people.

Six years later, the oil and gas business turned around and started booming. The Hope Field had paid out, so I had an income. One of my former Shell associates was working for the Rothschild Intercontinental Bank in London and wanted to fund a company for me and a partner. Rothschild purchased 30 percent of the stock and established a $1 million line of credit. My partner and I were very compatible, and our talents complemented each other. He managed the accounting and production, and I managed the exploration and land. Rule number seven: never take a partner unless his talents are required. In addition to my partner, we had a fourth shareholder who was a highly respected retired executive from Standard Oil Company in New Jersey. He and Rothschild gave us credibility both in the industry and in the financial community. We hired land men and geologists and started prospecting. Then we had to find the money to buy the properties and drill the wells. We made proposals to one hundred companies. For Vulcan Materials Corporation, our proposal was the thirty-fifth they had reviewed. Vulcan had hired a former Shell Vice President, for whom I had previously worked, to put them in the oil and gas business. With their consultants' recommendation, they contracted with us. Over the next four and a half years, we invested over $200 million and achieved an 18 percent rate of return for the investors. During that period, we bought out the Rothschild Bank for sixty times its investment. Our results so pleased the Vulcan board they insisted on buying our company.

Subsequently, the oil and gas business went into another depression. Many fortunes were lost, and over half the employees in the industry were laid off. The active drilling rig count went from 4,500 to about 800. During this time, I hired an outstanding young man to be the president of another company I had started that drilled low-risk development wells. We were successful in contracting with a utility company that wanted to get into the natural gas business. Again, we were able to hire outstanding technical people and succeeded in achieving attractive returns for our investor. History repeated itself and our investor bought our company for a favorable price.

After that sale, the president started up another company in which I was a significant owner. We were able to hire a fine staff and built up the reserves over several years. We recently sold that company into another rising market and are now looking for another opportunity.

In addition to the rules enumerated above, I am outlining other principles required to be an entrepreneur:

1. You must know your business well.
2. You must establish a reputation for honesty and integrity.
3. Starting your own business is very stressful. Make sure you have the temperament for it. Plan on one thousand sleepless nights.
4. Starting a business is not about good ideas. It's about the execution of good ideas. It's 90 percent management and 10 percent ideas. No successful investor will buy an idea.
5. When you are raising money for your business, you have to be open and reveal every detail of your business and your plans.
6. Don't be greedy. Your investors will require a significant part of the business, and if you want outstanding employees, you must be generous with them.

John A. Brock
Contributed by Heather Arena

KEY SUCCESS FACTORS: Integrity, Hiring Outstanding Talent, Executing Good Ideas

RECOMMENDED BOOKS: *Rules for Leadership, Life and Career* by John A. Brock

EDITOR'S NOTES: John A. Brock is an oil and gas company executive in Tulsa, Oklahoma. He graduated with a BS in Geological Engineering from the University of Oklahoma, served as an artillery officer in the Korean War, and spent some fifty years exploring and producing oil and gas. He serves on several boards of directors, is active in civic affairs, is a patron of the arts, and is an inductee to the Oklahoma Hall of Fame.

You have achieved success if you have lived well, laughed often, and loved much.
—*Anonymous*

NO MORE CHASING THE CARROT

PETE: I am sure everyone has had a carrot put in front of them and been told, "When you work harder, you'll get the carrot." But what you don't realize is you give up more of your life. Business or career—we forget it's a journey, not a destination. Are you enjoying your journey? We realize the only promises that are not broken in our lives are the ones we make to ourselves.

When I first met my wife, Kim, I told her we would own our own business and I couldn't work for anybody the rest of my life; and Kim said she felt the same way.

I grew up in a family business; five years after the business burned down and was relocated, it was failing. I was starting over at age twenty-six and with no college education. I began working for a national restaurant corporation in a management position, using my first job to educate myself with what it could teach me—from real estate to construction and on up. I worked my way into a regional position with several successful restaurant chains. My father, who had no education, inspired me. My parents owned a building that housed our restaurant, a pizza place, and a doughnut shop, along with sixteen apartments above the business. My father inspired me; but it is my wife, Kim, who motivates me.

KIMBERLY: I put myself through college working in retail from the age of sixteen and graduated with Degrees in Elementary Education and Early Childhood Education from Carlow University. Not long after graduation and teaching for a while, I realized I wanted more opportunity to express my creativeness, so I went back to retail. With my sales ability, I quickly became a director with Limited Inc. Victoria's Secret Beauty. My husband Pete spoke almost daily from the day I met him about the freedom of owning your own business and the glorious results of seeing the fruit of your talent, dreams, passion, risks, vision, tears, laughter, sweat, courage, soul, and determination. You will only get out of your business exactly what you put into it. If it was easy, then everyone could do it. Between the two of us, we have the perfect combination of extensive education and experience; and we enjoy each other's company, along with sharing eternal passion and determination—FAILURE IS NOT AN OPTION!

PETE: So after my wife and I left our jobs to open a restaurant/boutique, it was determined that I needed surgery for an injury to my leg from a previous car accident. The accident occurred three years earlier when I was returning from an operations review meeting for a national restaurant company and was involved in a four-car pileup on the Ohio Turnpike. I worked for approximately two years after the accident. I received constant therapy and ongoing noninvasive procedures. When the doctors said I couldn't travel anymore because it was hindering the success of the therapy and treatments, the company and I parted ways. This unexpected operation put our restaurant dream on hold, and we ended up living off our life's savings. With me being unable to work and my wife having already left her job, we had no income. And knowing nothing about the restaurant business, we were at a major crossroad in our lives and in our careers. But having experienced the stresses, lack of social life, and extreme workloads, along with travel in the corporate world, we both knew we would open a hot dog stand on the corner before we would ever work for anybody again.

We decided to press forward with part of the initial plan and opened a fashion accessory boutique called Serendipity: Accessories to Express Yourself. We started in a local hair salon, renting a sixty-eight-square-foot storage room to maximize impulse buys. Our restaurant designers designed this small room like a jewelry box. With our entrepreneur's attitude, we did all the remodeling ourselves, at a cost of $800, and opened Serendipity with an inventory of $1,600. We chose our name because *serendipity* means the art of finding the unusual or pleasantly unexpected through chance or sagacity. An accident and all that followed, fortunately, changed our lives for the better.

We discussed what we wanted to do and mapped out exactly where we wanted to take our business with expansion and growth. We had the same vision: no matter how small we started, we would build a company committed to service, quality, and execution. We also committed to each other if we couldn't agree on something, we would agree to disagree and move on until we did; and we wouldn't discuss work at the end of our workday so we could enjoy the quality of our life.

Opening the business on limited funds made it more challenging, and no banks would help us until our business had been open for two years. So we managed, with many sacrifices, on credit cards and keeping track of where every penny was and where it was going. Kim worked the first location alone because of its extremely limited size of sixty-eight square feet. While I recovered from surgery, I worked at home building our Web site and handling the financials. Kim built the business with her vibrant personality, fashion sense, and charisma, along with her passion for quality, service, and execution. Eventually, we started to become a store destination. In our second year, we opened our second location—1,200 square feet on a second level of a boutique/business building with rent we could afford. Now Kim and I were working together. As we continued to build our business, we looked for other opportunities.

Marketing! Our goal was to keep building our business, to produce our own product and to have a business on the street level. To do that, we had to get our name out there and keep it buzzing. With no outside visibility, we did local, low-cost marketing and networking through hotels, restaurants, colleges, convention centers, an e-mail list, and MySpace, along with opportunities on local TV shows doing fashion segments. We also advertised along busy walking areas, such as public transit shelters, and participated in local fashion shows and charity events.

In the store, we host quarterly fashion events at lunch from 11:00 a.m. to 2:00 p.m., featuring designers and their products, along with incorporating local makeup artists for mini makeovers, local nail salons for manicures, and local hair talent for consultations complimentary to our clients and at no cost to us because the consultants have a chance to market themselves. Everyone wins and gains new clients and boosts sales—plus, who doesn't like a little pampering while they shop and see what is hot for the season!

In February of 2009, we had been open for five years. We have moved our business to street level in a growing tourist spot, and have introduced our own lip—plumping gloss line called lipFUEL, which we plan to take nationwide this year, all the while continuing to build and grow Serendipity: Accessories to Express Yourself and our e-commerce business.

Kim and I will tell you if you work as hard for yourself as you do for others, your rewards will be greater. And if you go into business with the thought of failure, invest your time and money elsewhere. We can honestly say we love and enjoy what we are doing along our journey.

Pete and Kimberly Coppola

KEY SUCCESS FACTORS: Integrity, Passion, Consistency, Determination, Continuing Education, Being Positive

RECOMMENDED BOOKS: *Good to Great* by Jim Collins, *Leadership and the One Minute Manager* by Kenneth H. Blanchard, Patricia Zigarmi, Drea Zigarmi, *Who Moved My Cheese* by Spencer Johnson, MD

WEB SITE: *www.serendipityaccessories.com*

EDITOR'S NOTES: Peter and Kim are proud sponsors of Miss Pennsylvania USA, Miss Pennsylvania Teen USA, Miss West Virginia USA, Miss West Virginia Teen USA, and many local and national charities. They have recently been recognized in *Accessories*, a national industry magazine for impulse sales strategy, and were featured in the March '09 *Accessories* magazine for their influence on fashion.

CHAPTER TEN

PERSEVERANCE IS THE KEY

> *Perseverance is a positive, active characteristic. It is not idly, passively waiting and hoping for some good thing to happen. It gives us hope by helping us realize that the righteous suffer no failure expect in giving up and no longer trying. We must never give up, regardless of temptations, frustrations, disappointments, or discouragements.*
> —Joseph P. Wirthlin

The difference between the impossible and the possible lies in a person's determination.
—*Tommy Lasorda*

HE HAD CLIENTS—I HAD CREDIT

I knew something was up the afternoon my boss walked into the office at 2:00 p.m. and asked, "Wanna go have a beer?" It turned out we were both looking for new jobs. He because he and his partners no longer shared a common vision; me because his partners and I had never shared a common vision. Two minutes into the meeting over beer, he asked if I would leave the law firm to go with him to start a new one. Then he offered to make me an equal partner. I was thirty-three years old, had no clients of my own, had no business training, and had no background in running a business—my own or someone else's.

I consulted with my dad's elderly lawyer friend in Hugo, Oklahoma, who to this day laughs that there is nothing he knows more about than starting a law firm in Houston! However, he gave me great advice, "You're young, and you don't have much money. If it doesn't work out, you won't have lost much, and you can find another job." He was right on both counts. I closed my eyes and jumped off the precipice. I had become an entrepreneur.

We started on a shoestring, including funding payroll the first two months with my credit card. I always say we were the perfect professional partnership: he had clients; I had credit. In addition to practicing law, I spent the first two years manning the phones and learning to run the billing software. By the time we could afford a professional office manager, I almost understood the intricacies of business accounting, but can't say it was ever easy for me. Despite the cost, we hired an outside firm to handle payroll and taxes. We also hired a CPA, as well as a business lawyer, on the theory that a lawyer who represents himself (or in this case, herself) has a fool for a client. It was months before we could take any money for ourselves, and even then, the amount was small. Nonetheless, the ability to control our destiny made the struggle worth it.

Fourteen years later, we have weathered everything from being replaced by a cheaper competitor to enduring legal reforms that made us largely irrelevant. We survived changes in the business climate that resulted in a roller-coaster ride of economics—mostly toward the bottom loop of the roller. The worst day of my life was Monday, April 16, 2000, when our largest—essentially our only—client called to inform us they had gone bankrupt, owing us months and months of outstanding invoices. After going to the courthouse to tell the judge I was no longer going to be a participant in the ongoing trial, I came back to the office. We informed our lawyers and support staff we were going to have to lay all of them off because we did not have work for them to do, or hope of getting any quickly. The rent was paid for the month, and the computers were available; so they could stay until we were kicked out, but we couldn't afford to pay them. I made it through the speech without breaking down, then went to my office for a nice, deep sobbing cry before getting on the phone and trying to find new jobs for my now-ex-employees.

Fortunately for me, a new client called that same day, and we landed an interview for something new before I could get all my people placed. The new people came to interview us the following Wednesday, when we had only five actual employees. But we had called each of our former employees and asked if they would be willing to come and sit at their desks for the day. We would pay them for their time if we got hired, but couldn't afford to if we didn't. I have never been so gratified as that day. All but two of them (who had already started new jobs) came for the presentation. One of those who came took a day off from her other job to come sit at her desk. The presentation went well, the client loved our employees, we got hired, we paid all those who came for dress rehearsal, and both life and business continued. The bankrupt client is still in bankruptcy almost ten years later. We are still owed a fortune that we may never get, but the experience made us resilient and determined. We have weathered other events; fortunately, none that catastrophic. But the experience taught us to not put all our work with one client, no matter how insistent the client might be.

Over time, we added people and partners, many of them women. As a result, a few years ago, the firm became certified as a women-owned business. That certification has given us an opportunity and a platform for encouraging other women to take the plunge and jump into business themselves. I participate in many seminars and activities around the country, focusing strongly on the need for women lawyers to develop businesses of their own. I have spoken to a variety of audiences, not just lawyers, on the necessity of being able to support your own business without having to rely on someone else.

All these years later, my original male partner and I are still business partners, and we have weathered many, many storms. We have offices in both Texas and Maryland. Our firm has a national reputation and a book of clients based not just around the country but around the world. We continue to face difficult market circumstances and to work through them. Our firm has had as many as 125 employees and as few as five. No phase of business has been easy, but each has been educational in its own way.

The biggest difference between when we started and now is that now, I also have clients, and we both have credit. I would jump off the precipice again in a heartbeat, even knowing what I did not know then. I really believe hard work, focus, and determination make a difference. If I could return to the past and change something, I would take a few business classes in college and be more strategic in my business plan; but the business has worked out pretty well despite those deficiencies, so I am not sure I would change much.

Sharla J. Frost

KEY SUCCESS FACTORS: Perseverance, Determination, Work Ethic, Focus

RECOMMENDED BOOKS: *Brand You* by Tom Peters, *Freakonomics* by Steven D. Levitt, *The Tipping Point* by Malcolm Gladwell

WEB SITE: *www.powersfrost.com*

EDITOR'S NOTES: Sharla J. Frost calls Houston her home base. She is the managing partner of Powers & Frost LLP, a boutique litigation firm with offices in both Houston, Texas, and Towson, Maryland. When not on an airplane or in a courtroom, she spends as much time as she can at Frogsailles, her ranch property in Frogville, Oklahoma, where she has a boyfriend, a herd of cattle, and a motley collection of cats.

I am blessed that the big guy helps me. And blessed to have figured out I cannot do it on my own.
—*Scott Klososky*

THE HEAD AND THE HEART OF THE ENTREPRENEUR

I would like to say being an entrepreneur is easy. I would love to tell you it is a most noble pursuit and in the end, all the struggles are worth it. In fact, I would dearly love to tell you if you are reading this right now, you have what it takes to build your own business. Let's be real, though. It is a complicated game. With that said, here is my story.

I have the typical entrepreneur background—a tough family life growing up forced me to work full-time at the age of fifteen. During this time, I saw firsthand how a person with an idea could develop a company. The son of the founder of the company I worked for (illegally because I was underage) decided to start his own business and asked me to gather some of my friends and provide slave labor to assemble the product. I got paid extra for running the crew and was blessed to see firsthand how a business can be started from scratch.

I disliked school and could not convince myself I needed more at eighteen. I skipped college and worked my way up through a company for seven years. When my employer could no longer figure out how to finance the growing accounts receivables we were generating, I had the chance to buy the computer division I had been building. So there I was, a twenty-five-year-old self-taught computer guy with no experience, running my own business and pretty sure I would be the next technology zillionaire. I built my PC sales company up to a $40-million-a-year run rate—all on debt financing—and life was good. Right up until it was not. The problem, I learned, is borrowing money to finance the fast growth I had experienced was fine until things started going backwards. When revenue dips, you have a hard time paying off debt, and so I found myself at thirty years old with a very large lawsuit and a bankrupt company. After three years of lawsuits and filing Chapter 11, I sold the remaining pieces of the business, settled the suits out of court, and was able to get on with my life.

After this experience, many people might have just gone to work for a large company, where they don't make you put up your house as collateral, but not me. I had a taste of what it meant to build a company from a dream to reality, and I wanted more. I was much more humble and had learned thousands of valuable lessons about what it takes to start a business and guide it to financial success. So I started another business, and another; and the rest, as they say, is history, because every company since the first one has been a success. I could go into details, but that would be really boring. In the end, describing my wins is not important. We always learn a lot more from our failures than our successes because when we make mistakes, we know for sure what not to do.

With that in mind, I would like to share some observations about the process of building organizations. I believe building businesses is a very noble act. It employs people, supplies products, boosts the economy, and is what has made the U.S. economy the powerhouse it is. It takes guts and fortitude to build a business, or naïveté, I suppose. I always compare building companies to bull riding. When you ride a bull, you get hurt—even when you win, it hurts. It is not like golf where, win or lose, you get to be outside on the nice grass in your good clothes. I know this because I actually rode a bull once in a big rodeo. I loved riding the bull even though he threw me off and stepped on me. And I love building businesses even though it is hard. I am addicted to it, and even when I think I have built my last one, I am back in the game. There is no greater arena in which to measure oneself. It is a clear pass-or-fail test, where I take tons of risk, have to play hard for years, and then something happens. I get to sell the business and make lots of money, or . . . well, let's not discuss that option. If you really want to know what you are made of, being an entrepreneur is the ticket.

In order to share all my thoughts on the recipe for success, I would have to write an entire book. Success can most easily be predicted by the heart—not the mind—of the entrepreneur. There are millions of smart people in the world with good ideas. Very few of them have the discipline, determination, and moral code to win the game. I would much rather bet on a hard worker who never gives up than a smart person with little fortitude. When the tough days come, only the determined keep going. When there are one thousand decisions and tasks to get done, it is the disciplined person who performs. Too many first-time entrepreneurs believe their great idea will win the day. In reality, a great leader with a mediocre idea will win most of the time, while a poor leader will not succeed even with the best business plan in the world. If you want to know if you'll win, just look inside. All by yourself, stare into the mirror, and evaluate what you see. Forget what is in your head and go with your heart. That will tell you your odds.

Scott Klososky

KEY SUCCESS FACTORS: Over-The-Horizon Vision, Determination, Strong Work Ethic, Moral Grounding

RECOMMENDED BOOKS: The Bible, *Accelerando* by Charles Stross

WEB SITE: *www.klososky.com, www.technologystory.com*

EDITOR'S NOTE: Scott Klososky has been growing technology companies for more than twenty years. He sold his last company for $115 million. He helps his clients win in the market by reorganizing the way they implement technology as a tool to help them better see the future. He then goes farther by helping people understand how the cultural changes driven by the new generation of employees hitting the market can be an asset instead of an anchor.

The miracle, or the power, that elevates the few is to be found in their industry, application, and perseverance under the promptings of a brave, determined spirit.
—*Mark Twain*

LIVING WITH THE ENTREPRENEURIAL BUG

At the tender age of eight, a self-diagnosis revealed I had a daunting disease, the entrepreneurial bug! I remember precisely the day I caught it. I was eight years old and the proud owner of a Super Nintendo, which I had outgrown. I knew my parents had paid a lot for it and I realized it must have value to someone else. I called the local *PennySaver* magazine and placed a free thirty-word ad: "Super Nintendo for Sale, In Good Condition, $80, Call William" along with my contact information. Within days, a gentleman showed up at my house. I showed him my system, he paid me $80, and the deal was done. Not bad for a little work.

Just two years later, signs of entrepreneurship surfaced again. After learning to make stress balls in class, I came home and started a mini stress-ball-manufacturing and sales organization in my mom's kitchen. I used rice and flour to fill water balloons. Then I multilayered more water balloons with cut-outs on top which gave them a nice polka-dot design. Even without fully understanding the power of customer satisfaction at ten, I customized stress balls for customers who wanted them in their favorite colors. Within days, every friend and family member had one of my stress balls. I sold them for 50¢, $1, or whatever I could get generous people to pay. I was in business! The total revenues were around $100. I strategically hid this nest egg in my room, making sure to protect my capital for the future.

During my teens, symptoms of entrepreneurship began to appear again, and I absolutely had to treat them. I saw a need for a dog walker for working families. Dog walker or pooper scooper—call me what you like—I did it with a smile! I started walking Dudley, a beautiful golden retriever for $10 per week. Ensuring the dog did its business and then cleaning up the mess wasn't the most exciting part of my job, but the entrepreneurial bug was much stronger than picking up dog doo-doo. Neighbors started to spread the word and soon I had more dogs than I could handle. I did what any thirteen-year-old entrepreneur would do—hired my girlfriend and a friend to help. It was a simple business. I charged $2 per walk and paid my employees $1, while I handled responsibilities like revenue collection, client relationships, and scheduling. Friday evenings were my favorite time of the week. My customers rang my door bell one by one, delivering their weekly payment for my dog-walking services.

Looking back, my early ventures were somewhat comical. At nineteen years of age, I was diagnosed with full-blown entrepreneurship. My brother Mike stumbled across an article about a new concept, an eBay store where people bring their stuff and it's sold on their behalf. He shared the article with me and my other brother George, and I immediately fell in love with the idea. It reminded me of other successful companies created around things consumers are capable of doing but they would rather not bother with them, so they hire a service. I knew selling on eBay was a lot of work but we agreed it was a business we wanted to start.

The first hurdle was the discouragement we experienced from our family. As my brothers and I were reviewing our franchise agreements, signing them and stuffing them into FedEx envelopes, my sister-in-law told my brother, "You've got a great job". She also told me, "You have such a great career ahead of you as a CPA." My father consistently told us it was a silly business and would never work out. When we discussed the concept with friends and family, nobody seemed to fully understand it. "You mean it's a *real* store where I take my stuff?" Ummm, yes, exactly. EBay had done such a great job positioning itself as the virtual shopping mall that people couldn't believe real brick-and-mortar stores existed. In spite of all this discouragement, we saw incredible potential and wanted to get involved in this groundbreaking opportunity. We wanted a chance to be pioneers of change and help people alter their thinking about used and unwanted possessions. The discouragement we encountered was very nearsighted, but our vision was farsighted.

One of our first requirements was to be part of a brand name. We wanted to side with the market leader. During our due diligence, several companies were franchising the eBay drop-off store concept. We found iSold and were confident it would emerge as market leader in this category. (Just four years later, our belief was confirmed as we saw other franchisors go out of business.) The company iSold was started by the founders of Wetzel's Pretzels, a successful franchisor of several hundred stores. The founders had a background in marketing which we felt was missing in our own backgrounds. We went forward investing in this idea with incredible potential. What if my sister-in-law and my father were right? What if this became the worst decision I ever made? The unknown was scary but we would be teamed up with the market leader and have a good shot at success.

The next four years proved to be a wild ride on a very emotional roller coaster. Most people go into business with the fantasy of owning a business while they sunbathe in Tahiti. For me, another part of the fantasy was thinking cash flow comes quickly and it keeps flowing with minimal effort. Over the last few years, this fantasy adjusted and readjusted to reflect reality. The truth is the entrepreneur's reality can include an absolutely amazing Monday, followed by the worst Tuesday, which is then followed by a Wednesday even better than the best Monday. It's a constant emotional roller coaster with highs so high they make you scream out loud and lows so low they make you never want to be there again.

Our first year in business was the best time of my life! I spent most of the year traveling the world, and money flowed to my bank account faster than I could spend it. I was living the true entrepreneur's dream. Somebody pinch me, please! Unfortunately, it was a dream, and the reality was more like this: After finding our franchisor, we quickly moved through the phases of starting a corporation, raising capital, finding our first location, securing a lease, and building the retail store. During this time, I went from being a typical college student with a part-time job to being a nighttime college student running a full-time business. My grades tumbled from straight As to Cs. I was overworked, frustrated, and disappointed in myself. I couldn't sleep at night. My mind ran wild with the lists of things I had to do. The emotions I was experiencing often seemed unbearable. To top it off the business was in the red about $10,000 per month! So how does an entrepreneur keep going forward under these conditions? Simple. Along with all this pain and misery, we still had what we started with—a great idea and incredible potential. So I put my college education on hold for a semester in an effort to focus fully on the business. The business was my baby and there was no way I would allow it to fail.

Without a doubt, our first year was spent learning and readjusting our expectations. I was twenty years old and had to quickly learn how to hire and manage people twice my age. Some employees disrespected me and lied to me. I kept them longer than I should have and was too afraid to let the bad ones go. It seemed easier to put up with them than to hire and train new employees. Today I know better. I also had no formal training in marketing but suddenly became the marketing chief of our business. I said yes to every advertising sales rep that walked into my store. I didn't know about business systems and processes. I didn't know how to design them let alone implement them. I had to learn everything as I went along. It was chaotic and wild; each day was a new experience with something going wrong. But somehow, we managed to survive our first year in business, a time when many new businesses fail.

The second and third years were about improvement and fine-tuning the business. It took about a year for me to know my business and its inner workings on a deeper level. Most importantly, I recognized our weaknesses and how to learn and change from them. Day by day, improvement by improvement, we implemented new ideas. We improved our advertising strategy, increased our service fees, offered new services, and completely changed our staffing model. In the meantime, to our advantage, we saw our direct competitors shut their doors. We simply worked on improving our business as we absorbed more and more market share from closing competitors.

There is no one particular moment, thing, or event that changed the landscape of our business. It was simply the total accumulation of many tiny positive improvements that helped us outlast our competitors. Finally, toward the end of our third year, we saw the fruits of our labor begin to materialize in the form of financial rewards—still not enough to charter yachts or sunbathe in Tahiti, but better than paying to go to work each day. The business was still far from our original expectations but showed so much potential. We had a customer base that loved our services, qualified and talented employees, and many improvements in mind.

However, on disappointing days I wondered about the grass on the other side of the fence. It seemed very green and I questioned whether entrepreneurship was something I really wanted. For validation, I took an internship with a CPA firm to get a sense of what it was like to have a full-time job. It wasn't easy telling my partners I would be taking a three-month leave from our business. Overnight, I went from managing a million dollars of revenue, ten employees, and two stores to making copies for someone else's gain. Although the view was nice from the twentieth floor by the copy machine, I felt out of place. I wanted to fully experience this job, so I went through the entire summer working for someone else. I was told where to be and what time to be there. I was "spoken to" when I made mistakes. Overall, it was a good experience. The firm was good to me and the people I met were great. However, it didn't feel right working for someone else.

In a final effort to solve my confusion between entrepreneurship and a job, I consulted with my accounting professor at school. Her advice was completely the opposite of what I expected. She asked me, "How will you feel one day when you are the accountant doing work for your entrepreneurial clients who are really making the money?" At that exact moment, with just the two of us in the classroom, I had my epiphany. I realized I would always regret it if I threw away this opportunity. I decided 100 percent that entrepreneurship was my calling. Just as it takes many years to become a valuable professional, likewise it takes years to build a successful business. It was too early for me to quit, and the only way to beat my entrepreneurial bug was to give in to it entirely.

This was the last class of my college career and I graduated successfully with a Degree in Accounting and Business. Suddenly, I could focus entirely on my business—no homework in the evenings and no group projects on the weekends. I was certain with this added time and focus; we could be really successful and take our business to the next level.

Today we continue to work each day to implement new ideas and improvements that lead to growth. Owning our business has been more difficult than I ever could have imagined. I sometimes wonder whether, if I had known exactly what entrepreneurship would be like, I would have done it anyway. The challenges we have overcome seem even bigger in hindsight. One main success factor that continues to drive me forward is perseverance. What I have always envisioned hasn't happened yet. I need to keep doing what I'm doing until it does. For now, I go back to work, dreaming of those pleasant days in Tahiti.

I urge you, self-diagnosing entrepreneur, to give in to your condition if you seek to cure it. Let go of your fears entirely, because you can always lose something and get it back twice as quickly with your newfound knowledge and experience. Understand it is our human nature to fear failure. The *only* way to overcome this fear of failure is to actually do it. Prove to yourself and any who dare to doubt you that it can be done. Go forward, full forward!

William Fikhman

KEY SUCCESS FACTORS: Perseverance, Providing Value

RECOMMENDED BOOKS: *Rich Dad Poor Dad* by Robert Kiyosaki, *Think and Grow Rich* by Napoleon Hill, *Good to Great* by Jim Collins

WEB SITE: *www.877isoldit.com*

EDITOR'S NOTES: William Fikhman resides in Los Angeles, where he has spent most of his life. He holds a Bachelor of Science Degree with honors from California State University, Northridge, with an emphasis in accounting and business. Between meeting with clients and managing his business, Fikhman always makes time to maintain a balanced lifestyle. He enjoys spending time with family and friends. He has a serious passion for great food and enjoys traveling the world. He also enjoys reading books and magazines on various business topics.

A wise man will make more opportunities than he finds.
—*Francis Bacon*

IT HAPPENS BECAUSE I SAY SO

The morning of my thirtieth birthday, I thought to myself there has to be more. I had always gravitated toward successful young people, and others wondered how I had accomplished so much at a young age. I thought about all the amazing young people I had met over the years. I started researching, thinking there were some incredible stories out there most of the world didn't know about and would love to hear.

I wondered what would be the best way to get out the stories of these amazing young geniuses. Then it hit me—make a movie! I loved the idea . . . only, I had never made a movie before and didn't know how. But I knew I could do anything in this world, and if I let this chance pass me by, I would never get over it. I am all about taking action and seizing opportunity, and I knew this was the direction my path was meant to go . . . or at least I said so! I believe you don't *find* your destiny; you *define* your destiny.

I began to intensely research every aspect of the film world, from preproduction to postproduction to marketing to distribution. I was like a mad scientist, researching around the clock as if I was coming up with a cure for cancer. After about two months of research, I began the preproduction phase of the YES movie. I could have been nervous, but decided to be excited at every step of the way from interviewing production companies to arranging our shots to setting up a three-month tour of the United States of America.

I was fired up and ready to meet the nation's most successful self-made young multimillionaires as the production crew and I took off around the country. I look back now and think about all the amazing people I met along the way, and each person taught me so much about business and life and true happiness. As a first-time film producer, I felt very happy I made it to the production phase. Many filmmakers and people who want to start their own business never see their dream come to fruition for various reasons, but the biggest excuse I hear is that they don't have the money.

I can tell you that *"whatever* your dream is, there is always money out there to make it a reality!" If you want coaching on how to find the funds, you will have to watch our movie, *www.theYESmovie.com*. I could tell you everything went perfectly, because I believe everything did—even though we went over budget, we got lost, we missed appointments, we missed flights, equipment broke, we were stuck in traffic, blah, blah, blah, blah!

None of that matters. What matters is I spent three months on the road and got the footage I needed and *it rocked*. As we went into the postproduction phase, I was fortunate to hook up with Emmy-Award-winning writer Robyn Symon and Lifestyle Production guru Bernard Bonomo. With this awesome combination, our film was sure to be world-class.

Again, I could tell you about the challenges in the relationship, rearranging our schedules, or losing data in computer crashes, and the challenges of setting the strategy to make this the best film ever made on the topic of young entrepreneurship; but as you will learn when you watch the film, successful entrepreneurs all go through stuff, and it's not what matters. It's how you react to it that matters. What I did was make a world-class film despite all the stuff that happened along the way.

We are finishing up postproduction and putting on the final touches of this revolutionary film and have just hired the best public relations firm in the world—Stellar Communications, headed by Kate Romero and John Stellar. These two highly conscientious PR alchemists will connect the dots to make this film into a worldwide phenomenon.

As more and more media outlets are beginning to spotlight my journey and the story of the other amazing young entrepreneurs in our film, the world is beginning to open its mind to looking at what is possible for young persons in terms of making a positive impact in the world and taking ownership of their destiny.

If you are even remotely thinking about starting a business or want to bring your existing business to the next level, you must join the Young Entrepreneur Society and see the film that started this society. If you are still reading this, you know I am talking to you! You have made it this far; don't turn back. You are on the right path. Trust yourself and your creativity and genius within; it was divinely put there. I would love to hear all about you becoming the next *young entrepreneur*! Enjoy the YES movie at *www.theYESmovie.com*. We also have a social networking site at *www.YoungEntrepreneurSociety.com*.

Louis Lautman

KEY SUCCESS FACTORS: Commitment, Perseverance

RECOMMENDED BOOKS: *The Greatest Salesman in the World 1 & 2* by Og Mandino, *The Celestine Prophecy* by James Redfield, *The Alchemist* by Paulo Coelho

WEB SITE: *www.theYESmovie.com,
www.YoungEntrepreneurSociety.com*

EDITOR'S NOTES: Louis Lautman lives in South Beach, Florida, and spends his time empowering and inspiring a young generation of entrepreneurs.

It's not so important who starts the game but who finishes it.
—John Wooden

KEEP SWINGING—AN ENTREPRENEUR'S STORY OF OVERCOMING ADVERSITY AND ACHIEVING SMALL BUSINESS SUCCESS

A lot of entrepreneurs will tell you stories of how early on they had some sort of eureka moment that was the catalyst to start their business. It would be nice if I could tell you a similar story. But the truth is, I started my company, Interactive Solutions Inc. (ISI) after I got *fired*. Worst yet, it was on my thirty-ninth birthday! It was a tough time because not only had I lost my job, but it happened a few weeks before Christmas. When the initial shock and anger wore off, I then had to step back and realize I had a family to support and needed to get back in the saddle. The biggest challenge in the start-up year was trying to put together a business plan for a technology company without a computer. After scrambling around for a few weeks, I was able to cobble together a very rough (six-page) plan that had the financial pro forma hand typed on a Franklin planner column sheet. It wasn't pretty, and truthfully, all of the banks around Memphis laughed at me when I presented it to them; but weeks later, it got me an audience with some local private investors. I'm not sure to this day whether the investors really understood my plan or just felt sorry for me; but in March 1996, they provided the initial seed money, and that's how ISI got off the ground.

ISI started to really grow after our first year, which was good and bad. The good part was we were selling more video conferencing systems than we did in our start-up year ($260,000 to $1 million). The bad part was the company was having serious growing pains that were jeopardizing our future. Part of the problem was the key company support engineer (who was also my partner) was located in a remote office, which was three hours away in Kentucky. We struggled almost daily with a host of issues that included logistics, cost overruns, customer complaints, etc.

My first instinct was to consolidate our efforts and have my partner move to Memphis, where we could save money and build the company together. Sounds good? It did to me, but not to him; and that was the problem. Kentucky was his home, and he was not about to move. We were at a stalemate. Now what? Since he owned 50 percent of the company, the short answer was I had to buy him out. Just write him a check and be done with it, right? Except I had no more money in January of 1998 than I did in March of 1996. Did I want to risk everything and put my family in possible bankruptcy to chase my crazy dream? I started to wonder what my customers, partners, and suppliers would think. Was the engineer the real brains behind the company? I had awful sweaty nightmares about all my customers leaving me at once. Even when I woke up, I felt cold and clammy; it still felt like it was happening, like it was real. Doubt can be a nasty enemy. I ended up pulling the money together with a ridiculously complicated bank loan. For the first time in my career, I felt like I finally had control of my company and my future.

The company grew dramatically over the next four years to over $6 million in revenue with record profits by the end of 2002. Things seemed to really be going well, or at least we thought so. Then on April 29, 2003, literally the day after I read an article in *Inc.* magazine about embezzlement, I discovered a theft at ISI of over $257,000 within our payroll and accounts payable department. Unbelievable! But the numbers didn't lie. My accounting manager had written herself and the receptionist commission/bonus checks for over $47,000, with an additional $210,000 in forged checks that went through our accounts payable department. It felt like it was the day my business almost died, and was made worse by the fact it happened just ten months after my older brother had suddenly died. How bad was it? I felt like I was literally staring at the abyss. But it was also a time for decisions. How do I handle this? The following is an excerpt from my book *Keep Swinging*.

> What were my options? This was humiliating, a potential disaster if my employees find out. It might sink the company. What about my clients and vendors? Could I afford to confront this in public like the Graffs did? (*Inc.* magazine) Could I afford not to? I'm used to making decisions. Fast. I've never been patient, I'm hyper, and I wear my emotions on my sleeve. I'm also a man of faith, and I've never raised my hand to my own children. But I've never shied away from a fight, and I am not about to now. The stakes are just too high—my employees, their families, my family, and my soul. I have given everything to this business, and now this woman wants to take it away. I won't let her. So I do what I do best. I act.

Immediately, I got some help from the U.S. Secret Service; and over the course of the next several months, we had the accounting manager arrested and put in prison for over eight years. Even today, I look back on this truly surreal experience and still feel fortunate to have been able to survive. The best part was the next year (2004), ISI not only survived, we doubled sales to over $10 million—pretty inspiring stuff for a company that was almost out of business the year before.

In looking back on the start-up and growth of ISI, I think it has been so much more rewarding than other small business success stories because the path to get there has not been easy. ISI has also recognized we have had a lot of local support along the way, which is why the company created ISI Gives Back. It is a program that allows ISI employees to request company contributions to charities of their choice. Other organizations such as the Boy Scouts, Junior Achievement, Better Business Bureau, and the American Cancer Society are also supported by ISI with board members, fund-raisers, etc. It's been ISI's experience by doing good in the community, it can also be good for your business.

Jay B. Myers

KEY SUCCESS FACTORS: Perseverance, Integrity, Passion, Work Ethic

RECOMMENDED BOOKS: *Keep Swinging: An Entrepreneur's Story of Overcoming Adversity and Achieving Small Business Success* by Jay Myers, *Road to Organic Growth* by Dr. Edward Hess, *So You Want to Start a Business?* by Dr. Edward Hess, *Only the Paranoid Survive* by Andy Grove, *Small Giants* by Bo Burlingham

WEB SITE: *www.isitn.com, www.keepswingingbook.com*

EDITOR'S NOTES: Jay B. Myers is Founder, CEO, and President of Interactive Solutions Inc. in Memphis, Tennessee.

KEY SUCCESS FACTORS

Key success factors listed after each story were compiled to determine those that the featured entrepreneurs deemed most important. The following are the top ten according to the number of times each was listed.

1. Passion
2. Perseverance
3. Work Ethic
4. Determination
5. Customer Service
6. Integrity
7. Taking Action
8. Relationships
9. Focus
10. Faith

The following *key success factors* were listed by more than one entrepreneur, but did not make the top ten list (in alphabetical order):

1. Adaptability
2. Confidence
3. Courage
4. Family Support
5. Finding a Niche
6. Having the Right Team
7. Hiring Outstanding Talent
8. Optimism
9. Positive Attitude
10. Vision

RECOMMENDED BOOKS

There were eighty-seven different books recommended by the featured entrepreneurs, yet only six made the list by two or more contributors. The six that received a recommendation by multiple entrepreneurs are the following:

- *Good to Great* by Jim Collins
- *Think and Grow Rich* by Napolean Hill
- *How to Win Friends and Influence People* by Dale Carnegie
- *Rich Dad Poor Dad* by Robert Kiyosaki
- *Who Moved My Cheese? An Amazing Way to Deal with Change in Your Work and in Your Life* by Spencer Johnson, MD
- The Bible

WATCH FOR VOLUME II OF A CUP OF CAPPUCCINO FOR THE ENTREPRENEUR'S SPIRIT

A Cup of Cappuccino for the Entrepreneur's Spirit features a series of books of entrepreneurs' true stories written to inspire, energize, and teach the reader. The stories include adversities, challenges, triumphs, and successes experienced by the entrepreneur to help readers discover passion and the basic principles for living the entrepreneurial dream.

The series will include Volumes I, II, and III of *A Cup of Cappuccino for the Entrepreneur's Spirit* and editions including a Women Entrepreneurs' Edition, an Internet Entrepreneuers' Edition, a Global Entrepreneurs' Edition, an Ecopreneurs' Edition, a Social Entrepreneurs' Edition, a Disabled Entrepreneurs' Edition, a Native American Entrepreneurs' Edition, a Hispanic Entrepreneurs' Edition, an African American Entrepreneurs' Edition, an Australian Entrepreneurs' Edition and others.

The format and guidelines for writing a story are located on my Web site at *www.acupofcappuccino.com*; click on Submit Story.

After reviewing the guidelines, please submit your story as a Microsoft Word document attached to an e-mail to *jeretta@acupofcappuccino.com*.

> Jeretta Horn Nord, Founder and CEO
> Entrepreneur Enterprises LLC
> *A Cup of Cappuccino for the Entrepreneur's Spirit*
> 601 S. Washington #105
> Stillwater, OK 74074
> 405-747-0320
> 405-743-4802 (fax)

Please send your reactions to the stories in this book. Which stories were your favorite, and what impact did they have on you?

HELPING FIRST-GENERATION ENTREPRENEURS

A portion of the proceeds from this book will be put in a fund to help first-generation entrepreneurs with start-up funds. Watch for details on the Web site:

www.acupofcappuccino.com